CURIOUS PLEASURES

A Gentleman's Collection of Beastliness

CURIOUS PLEASURES

A Gentleman's Collection of Beastliness

BEING A NARRATIVE OF MANKIND'S CURIOUS AND
CARNAL DEEDS AND PRACTICES; THE WHOLE FORMING A
VALUABLE, INTERESTING AND INSTRUCTIVE COMPENDIUM

most painstakingly compiled by
THE REV'D DR ERASMUS ST JUDE CROOM D.D.

EXTENSIVELY ILLUSTRATED

PUBLISHED IN LONDON, 1901

Published in 2007 by
Virgin Books
Thames Wharf Studios
Rainville Rd
London W6 9HA

Copyright © The Reverend Dr Erasmus St Jude Croom DD
2007

A catalogue record of this book is available from the British Library

ISBN 978 1 905264 13 1

The paper used in this book is a natural, recyclable product made from
wood grown in sustainable forests. The manufacturing process
conforms to the regulations of the country of origin.

Typesetting by Phoenix Photosetting, Chatham, Kent

Printed and bound by Mackays of Chatham, Chatham, Kent

1 3 5 7 9 10 8 6 4 2

LIST OF ILLUSTRATIONS

LIST OF ILLUSTRATIONS *cont.*

Author's Foreword

Learned gentlemen, it is with no small degree of trepidation that I present you this small work, for it contains much discussion of that which we could wish was no part of human nature, the carnal desire inherent in man. Yet while such subjects are plainly unsuitable for those of delicate disposition, ladies and any who lack that clarity of mind which comes only upon receipt of a worthy education, it is my belief that they should be explored and understood, no less than any other subject. Thus, I have taken it upon myself to perform this disagreeable task, devoting my life to such studies, the results of which I now present for your instruction.

Nor, I fear, do my researches relate solely to the male of the species. Womankind, the fairer and the gentler sex, stand to us upon a pedestal, pure and virtuous, unsullied by the temptations of the flesh to which man is heir, or at least, this is the case for a substantial proportion of ladies of good family and honest upbringing and indeed a not insignificant proportion of their less highly placed sisters, but it is not, I regret to say, by any means universal. Already I hear the cries of condemnation, and gentlemen, believe me, nothing would gladden my heart more than to learn that I am wrong, but a man of science must confront empirical fact just as the sailor confronts the towering wave or the soldier his enemy's steel and fire. Thus I am obliged to reveal a distressing fact, that the daughters of Eve, no less than the sons of Adam, can succumb to the temptations of debauchery.

This work has been no light task. I am now in my seventy-seventh year, and first began to consider applying scientific methods to the subject of carnality when still a curate at St Botolph's, in 1849. Since that date I have applied myself to the task with what I trust is proper Christian fortitude combined with that thirst for scientific truth which has done so much to make Britannia foremost among the world's nations. I have endured the imprecations of outraged householders, the assaults of indignant swains, the professional attentions of the Constabulary and the rebukes of innumerable ladies of both high and low station, all of whom have, at one time or another, mistaken my intentions and assumed that I belong to that very class of people whose licentious habits I seek to lay bare to public scrutiny.

Given the above circumstances, and after careful consultation with my legal advisers, I have chosen to grant anonymity to all those persons mentioned herein, without fear or favour. In doing so I am aware that I am laying myself open to claims of shielding the guilty, but it must be borne in mind that this is a work of science and not of detection, much less a collection of notes gathered to make the task of Her Majesty's police easier, as some have had the temerity to suggest it should be.

My findings will, I trust, prove of interest. They are certainly extensive, if nothing else, and I can without fear of contradiction claim to be the leading authority on these matters. In order to present such facts I have had no choice but to remark on subjects generally considered indecent and, in order to make my meaning clear, employ words not normally in polite usage. The reader should be aware of this and, I trust, will excuse such lapses of taste as I have been forced to make in the name of science and of truth.

I also offer the most profound apology for elements of my terminology, which I fully realise will make many a scholar shudder, and would have appalled my own mentors. If I have at times permitted certain curious constructions, and even the combination of Latin and Greek in the formation of words, pray be assured that this is neither through ignorance nor slovenly habit, but because the words in question have come to be used in common parlance by rakes, rogues and the depraved, who evidently know no better.

Thus armed, pray proceed.

The Rev'd Dr Erasmus St Jude Croom DD
The Rectory, S------ B-------, the eleventh of November, 1900

{A}

Ablutophilia

The curious association of carnal arousal with washing.

The true ablutophiliac can only become aroused during washing and in no other circumstances, but this is a rare condition. Mild ablutophilia, properly termed ablutolagnia, on the other hand, is remarkably common, especially among women. In general it is a solitary activity, although exceptions exist.

In the nature of washing it is necessary to disrobe, and therefore perhaps not altogether surprising that sexual hysterics have come to find it arousing. There is also the issue of hygiene, for which it is essential to touch the breasts, posteriors and yet more private parts, in particular the fundamental aperture, a process which carries an inevitable risk of stimulation. Having given in to her base instincts, the typical ablutophiliac is likely to spend some time soaping her breasts, with particular attention to the teats, before moving down to those most private of regions, again for the vigorous application of soap until she reaches a state of hysteria.

Ablutophilia is also related to voyeurism, in that washing provides men an opportunity to observe women undressing, *en déshabillé* or naked. This is a popular subject among pornographers, notably those who abuse the cinematographic art. For example, the brothers G------, of 6, Rue St Martin in Paris, have, across recent years, produced over forty short films, each showing a different young lady in the act of performing her ablutions. These follow an identical pattern, as the girl in question enters the bathroom, disrobes in a manner apparently casual but in practice carefully arranged so as to arouse maximum interest in the watching male, and bathes herself, always paying particular attention to the soaping of her breasts. In the thirty-seven examples I have recorded, only two variations on this theme were observed. Eight included the girl turning onto her front and lifting her posteriors above the level of the water for the purpose of soaping herself in that area, and in one the subject,

{Fig. 1} 'The consequences are inevitable'

having completed her bath, accompanies the process of towelling herself down with an act of flagrant onanism.

There is also an association between ablutophilia and exhibitionism, which, by contrast, is less the subject of commercial abuse than of private indulgence. An example is provided by Lady A---- T---------, who is in the habit of bathing thrice daily and declines to place a lock on her bathroom door on the plainly spurious grounds that locks are emblematic of mistrust and covetousness. The consequences are inevitable. *See fig. 1*

Agalmatophilia

A rare but ancient paraphilia in which the subject falls in love with a beautiful statue, as described in Ovid's *Pygmalion*, hence the vulgar term, pygmalionism. While undeniably peculiar, this practice has been argued to represent a quest for purity and perfection, thus raising it above more earthy erotic pleasures.

Sadly, the same cannot be said for the more common forms of agalmatophilia, of which there are three. Firstly, there is the almost exclusively female practice of using a statuette or doll as an aid in self abuse. The object is generally a model of an adored person, either a lover or somebody unobtainable in the flesh, but may simply be the nearest long, hard object to hand.

The second, and most beastly, instance is almost exclusively a male perversion and involves the substitution of a large doll for a woman. Such dolls are generally made of straw, dressed in female clothing and include a soft, penetrable object, such as an eviscerated chicken, placed so as to mimic the mouth or private parts. As one might expect, this is a predominately rustic practice and notably common in the county of Norfolk, also the Bresse region of France. Indeed, in the latter instance I once found myself obliged to provide consolation to the young wife of a Monsieur F----, who was upset both by her husband's habit of visiting the local scarecrows late

{Fig. 2} 'Helpless against the erotic advances of her partner'

at night in preference to their own marital bed and his insistence on taking a fresh chicken on each occasion, a practice she considered profligate.

In the third instance the object of affection is neither a statue nor a doll, but a living person feigning an inability to move. In most instances the male is active, the female passive, although roles may be reversed, but in either case the essence of the depravity is that the receptive partner maintain immobility and therefore can pretend to be entirely helpless against the erotic advances of her partner. It is common for the passive partner to be painted white, so as to resemble ivory or marble. A good example is provided by Lady F-------- B---------, who has been known to arrange the younger and more athletic among her footmen in the form of caryatids supporting bowls of fruits and pastries for the delectation of her guests. Her claim that this is merely an enhancement to her artistic salons is plainly false, or at the least not entirely truthful, as following each event she will thrash those who have moved and indulge her not inconsiderable carnality with whoever she feels has provided the best service. *See fig. 2*

Agastopia

Describes the practice of limiting the focus of erotic pleasure to a single part of the body rather than the whole. Eight common instances of agastopia are considered separately: the virile member and the female receptacle thereof, breasts, bellies, posteriors, legs, feet and hair. However, the phenomenon is not limited to the erogenous zones, nor to overtly erotic features. In addition to the eight commonest examples, the fetishisation of hands, eyes and mouths is most frequent, but it is probable that every body part has at some time been the focus of an erotic fetish. In some cases this can take on an almost religious fervour, and may be termed worship, hence my use of the suffix –adoria with respect to these practices.

An instructive example is that provided by Mr S---- R----- of King's Lynn in Norfolk, who, after spending his formative years engrossed in the spectacle of female eel catchers wading in the fens with their skirts raised but their lower legs submerged, became unable to gratify himself save in contact with his wife's knees.

Anapirophilia

An erotic fascination with invalids, or most frequently, with those who have had the misfortune to lose a limb, a practice as peculiar as it is beastly. It is also rare, and I have recorded only five examples, all male, although with so small a sample it would be wrong to conclude that the practice is restricted to that sex. However, all five have been men of cultivated tastes, which may well be significant.

In particular, anapirophiliacs generally have a highly developed sense of æsthetics, and will lavish hours of attention on perfecting the most minute detail of anything that relates to their penchant. Thus we have Lord C---- St C----, who would spend several hours each morning preparing his lady wife's wooden leg, first sanding down any blemishes that might have occurred and applying new varnish, then painting the toenails and applying a trifle of rouge to the upper thigh, before putting on a stocking, a garter belt and a shoe, all with loving care. Lady St C----, incidentally, had little interest in this process, and would habitually detach her leg after a few minutes and go about her business on a crutch until he was finished.

More curious still was the case of Colonel Sir R----- L-----, who married a lady of exceptional beauty but with neither legs nor arms, Miss B------- H-----. For over forty years he lavished every attention upon her, carrying her from place to place, dressing her and grooming her as if she were some exquisite doll. The Colonel's choice was always put down to Christian charity and solicitude, of which there may have been an element, but it should be noted that this was not his normal character. Indeed, as a military man he was a known martinet, and at Sobraon lost eight men out of every ten under his command. Rather, following close observation, I am convinced that his primary motive lay in her absolute helplessness, which enabled him to exert an otherwise unattainable degree of control, both in general, and more specifically during congress.

Androgyny

A regrettably common form of beastliness in which a man, or woman, instead of being content with the Lord's creation, chooses to adopt characteristics more typically associated with the opposite gender. This is often considered a characteristic of a decadent or pampered society, and such may indeed be the case, but in this volume we are concerned not with the cure, but with the symptoms. There is also considerable overlap between androgyny and transvestism, also lavenderism, both of which we will consider elsewhere.

The male androgyne may be identified by a smooth face, unusually long hair, effete mannerisms, unnatural delicacy, the wearing of strong scent or even cosmetics, and the absence of that robust vigour so characteristic of the Englishman. He is a dainty, over-particular individual, often to be found in the world of theatre or perhaps literary criticism, rather than wielding a lump hammer or riding to hounds. His carnal proclivities need no detailed examination, save to say that he probably extends his preference for the role God gave to the fairer sex to the marital bed, or wherever else may prove convenient.

The female androgyne, while rarer, also shows greater variation in form. We have, on the one hand, women such as the late Miss H----- S----, who by virtue of a robust physique and the misfortune of being pressed into the Royal Navy while dressed in the clothes of her brother-in-law, came to serve several years in the marines, including combat at the battle of Pondicherry. More typical, and more beastly by far, are those women of the sapphic persuasion who adopt a male guise in order

{Fig. 3} 'I watched from a distance, as befits the detached observer'

to facilitate the seduction of their unsuspecting sisters, an outrageous practice into which it has been my sad duty to conduct considerable research.

Perhaps the most instructive example I am able to provide is that of Lady A----- T----, daughter of the Duke of W-------. I first suspected her proclivities when I noticed her applying burnt cork to her face in order to create the impression that she wore a moustache. Somewhat later, I observed her in full evening dress, perfectly correct had it been on a man, but in the circumstances making a positively indecent display of her rounded posteriors, and in conversation with Miss R------ T----, whose blushing responses made it all too evident that she had been taken in by this wicked ruse. This I watched from a distance, as befits the detached observer, but when, to my horror, it proved that Lady A----- was not content with stolen kisses I was forced to intervene, and not before time, as my appearance allowed Miss R------ to escape with her virtue intact if not her modesty. *See fig. 3*

Aphrodisiac

B roadly speaking, anything that may cause carnal arousal, although the term is most frequently applied to comestibles, and more specifically those of a phallic or marisciac nature.

In many instances, this effect relates to purely visual stimulation due to the association of an object with the carnal act and therefore affects only those whose minds are already corrupted. Thus, while it is true that a lewd woman eating a stalk of asparagus can be sufficient to give even the most jaded of roués palpitations, persons of high moral rectitude have nothing to fear. Examples include, of the masculine trait: asparagus, avocado pears, bananas, carrots and strawberries; and of the feminine trait: apples, apricots, figs, oysters and peaches.

Certain otherwise innocent substances may also be used to produce excitement and therefore arousal, but again, only in those already susceptible. A virtuous woman is no more likely to surrender herself to beastliness when in high spirits than otherwise, although she might well be more likely to accept a respectable proposition. Here examples include ginger, honey, mustard, truffles, wine, vanilla and a wide range of more exotic foodstuffs, mainly of Chinese origin and, in my view, of highly dubious efficacy.

Lastly, there are a few substances which are in effect poisons in that they inflame the delicate tissues of the body, thus causing arousal, and so are dangerous both to the physical and moral wellbeing of those who consume them. Chief among these is the dried extract of certain coleopterous insects of the family *Meloidae*, a substance the infamous Comte d- S--- is said to have used as an aid to seduction, leading to his condemnation for poisoning and sodomy. This substance is also one of the ingredients of a Moroccan fruit paste known as dawamesk, which depraved persons of that country use for purposes of seduction, but which has recently become available at the establishment of Messrs J------ & P-------- in Jermyn Street, although at ten and six for a jar of no great size I do not think we need fear a sudden epidemic of lost virtue.

Apiolagnia

The use of bees for erotic stimulation, a most curious practice, as strange as it is debased, but which provides an excellent illustration of the ingenuity which the lewd employ in order to satisfy their desires.

On the afternoon of the tenth of June, 1888, I was observing the house of Colonel Sir J--- C-----, a known masochist and flagellant. Despite my existing knowledge of the Colonel's habits, I was surprised to see him venture from his house heavily shrouded but for his private parts. He was carrying in one hand a large pot of honey and in the other an ordinary domestic cane. I was yet more surprised when, on reaching the vicinity of his beehives, he proceeded to apply a liberal coating of the viscous liquid to his virile member.

I had already deduced that he was intending to perform some peculiar act, but I had not realised just how peculiar, nor how dangerous. Taking up the cane, he began to belabour the nearest beehive, while simultaneously applying vigorous stimulation to his member. His intention was clearly for the bees to attack his exposed parts, presumably with the intention of achieving emission, but given his advanced age and extreme corpulence I felt he was taking his life in his hands and was therefore forced to act.

Reasoning that the unexpected appearance of a man of the cloth would shame him into abandoning his act of lunatic onanism I stepped forth from the bushes and gave a polite cough to draw his attention to my presence. Unfortunately the result was not the one I had anticipated, for far from showing remorse he demanded to know what I was doing in his garden and even went so far as to threaten to assault me with both cane and honey pot. I am not a man easily browbeaten, and continued to remonstrate with him, upon which he attempted to carry out his threat. Given the condition he was in and the cloud of angry bees now surrounding him, I chose to retreat, although I am pleased to say that I maintained my composure sufficiently well to raise my hat as we passed two elderly ladies in the lane leading past the Colonel's house.

Aretifism

A somewhat obscure paraphilia relating not to the feet at such, but to their exposure and hence vulnerability. It is apparently confined to the male, or so my researches would seem to indicate. The typical aretifist is a harmless enough fellow, seeking only to admire ladies' naked feet, a habit which may be indulged either in privacy or at a seaside resort with no great consequence.

There are, however, exceptions, and more than one regrettable incident has been recorded. A certain Miss A------- T-------, for instance, while on a perambulation of

Wales, chose to lave her feet in a tarn, the day being warm and the apparent absence of onlookers negating any question of impropriety. Unfortunately an aretifist proved to be in the vicinity and stole her shoes and stockings so that he might enjoy the sight of her exposed feet and her vulnerability as she was obliged to walk a distance of some miles while barefoot.

Art

T he highest expression of the human soul save only for divine worship, when properly employed, but all too often an agency for corruption. For example, no man can view Michelangelo's David without a sense of awe for the artist's skill, and yet the statue is naked, his virility displayed for all to see. Can this be proper?

Under no circumstances would I wish to destroy or deface such a magnificent work of art, nor would I wish to curtail the liberties of artists in their choice of subject. However, let there be no question that the display of the naked body is ungodly and that such works should not be placed on public view for fear of corrupting the innocent, and in particular young ladies. We restrict the viewing of those books that contain improper passages to those with the maturity and education to view them without risk of inflamed passions, and the same should be true of all art, even the greatest.

I am not a proponent of the placing of clothes on statues, as a set of woollen combinations on the David or a chemise on the Aphrodite of Milos would simply look absurd, but would like to see galleries set aside for the housing of indecent works. These would include not only statuary and paintings, but literature, thus bringing together all such things in one place, making the exclusion of the unsuitable easier and facilitating the task of those who wish to conduct serious research.

Unfortunately, such a scheme is unlikely to be entirely efficacious due to the ease with which such works can now be reproduced and the determination of so many people to place artistic freedom before morality and common sense. Thus, Sir R------ B-----'s translations of *The Kama Sutra of V---------* (1883) and *The Perfumed Garden of the Cheikh Nefzaoui* (1886), although issued by private subscription only, can be obtained readily enough in London or even our provincial cities, and at no great cost. Nor when the French government, in a moment of rare morality, sought to ban those licentious poems penned by M. C------ B---------- as *Les Fleurs de Mal* (1857) were they particularly successful, as the same poems were promptly reproduced in Belgium, in a collection entitled *Les Epaves* (1866). Vastly more licentious are the works of the Comte d- S---, and yet despite the most dogged suppression they may be obtained with no great difficulty and often in splendid bindings.

If high art can corrupt, what of the low? This is a considerable problem in society, and is becoming more so as the rise of industry makes production and distribution cheaper. No longer must the pornographer labour for hours with pen and ink or his set of etching tools, when with the aid of an automatic printing press he may produce thousands upon thousands of copies of whatever depraved text or illustration he pleases. His lewd creations may then be taken to every part of the country within hours by the misuse of the train, and sold for a few pennies to rakes and seducers, strumpets and harlots.

The centre of this trade is, unsurprisingly, Paris, and the preferred medium of corruption the photograph. In my estimation there are at any given time some one hundred immoral or misguided young women posing in various states of undress or even naked and a corresponding number of photographers taking their pictures in that city alone. Nor is their production limited to simple nudity, but includes depictions of every conceivable form of beastliness.

Even in London, and despite the best efforts of the Metropolitan Police, it is possible to purchase lewd novelettes, often lavishly illustrated, and collections of improper pictures and photographs. Nor are these necessarily of low quality, but include detail to ensure that nothing whatsoever is left to the imagination, while they are produced in such quantity that new material becomes available on an almost daily basis. Thus was the late Mr H---- S------ A----- able to amass a collection of extraordinary volume, including many thoroughly licentious works he is said to have penned himself, but so rapid is the production of scandalous books nowadays, that his *Index Librorum Prohibitorum* was severely out of date even before it was printed. I see no evidence of this tide slackening, quite the reverse, and therefore it is my sad duty to predict that with the inexorable march of industry it is only a matter of time before our fair country becomes submerged beneath a tide of pornography.

Barbaphilia

An unhealthy erotic obsession with beards, or more generally, with bearded men. This is not a common paraphilia, possibly because the majority of women, even immoral women, find the tickling sensations associated with beards more irritating than otherwise.

Lavenderists experience no such difficulties, and it is among their number that the majority of barbaphiliacs are found. For some reason I have yet to fathom, such people are seldom content simply with a bearded man, but tend to prefer a number of associated characteristics: great height, considerable bulk and red or reddish brown hair, so that the ideal object of desire for the typical lavenderist barbaphiliac resembles nothing so much as a specimen of the grizzly bear (*Ursus ferox*).

Perhaps more curious still are the rare sapphic barbaphiliacs, such as Mlle H----- A---- of Perpignan in France. Her preference was for dashing, athletic individuals, but she was a true sapphist and therefore had no time whatever for men, a combination of tastes that led her to insist on her lovers applying cork to their faces so as to imitate a small, neat beard and a pair of sharp moustachios.

The female barbaphiliac also tends to have specialised tastes, and of an even more disturbing nature. Rather than showing a preference for the long, flowing beard that one might associate with patriarchal sagacity, or that neatly trimmed example favoured by the Prince of W----, she tends to seek out men whose beards are black and cut to a sharp point, and who are also stark bald. This might not appear unduly peculiar, until one considers that this is the appearance customarily associated with the devil.

Bellicolagnia

A potentially broad paraphilia involving the corruption of all things military for carnal purposes.

The typical bellicolagniac is an old soldier of the officer class, who, after a lifetime of drilling, inspecting and on occasion chastising his men develops a taste for debauched forms of these same practices. Interestingly, such men are very seldom lavenderists, and prefer the subjects of their depravity to be attractive young women, who all too frequently come to enjoy or even crave the same debaucheries.

No better example exists of this paraphilia than that of the fourth Lord G-----, who, during the later part of the eighteenth century, maintained an entire regiment of female soldiers, both officers and other ranks, each and every one of them supplied with a smart if notably lewd uniform consisting of a red coat, tight at the waist and cut at the front so as to accentuate the bosom, short and flared behind so as to reveal the seat of a pair of tight white canvas trousers cut to follow the exact contours of each girl's posteriors, smart boots of black leather, a white canvas belt much like a miniature corset, and a neat red cap adorned with a white plume. Elements of this uniform are said to have been abandoned on parade to a greater or lesser extent, and his Lordship is known to have been something of a fanatic for drill and inspection, even going to far as to employ a magnifying glass in order to allow him to detect minute imperfections in the girls' uniforms. *See fig. 4*

{Fig. 4} 'To employ a magnifying glass in order to allow him to
detect minute imperfections in the girls' uniforms'

Berkley Horse

A wooden frame invented by Mrs T------ B------ of Fitzrovia in order to facilitate the simultaneous flagellation and stimulation of clients at her various houses of negotiable virtue. Mrs T------ B------, it is said, was a true enthusiast for her trade, and of genuinely depraved character rather than purely mercenary. This character, combined with charm, common sense and discretion, made her something of a paragon among her contemporaries and her establishment of foremost popularity among the roués and rakes of the late Georgian era.

Her particular speciality was the birch, generally for use on her gentleman clients or one of the girls under her supervision, but very occasionally for herself. To this end she designed the device that has come to bear her name, an open frame of stout wooden members constructed so that it will remain in a stable, upright position during use. Adjustable leather straps allow the wrists and ankles of whoever has been chosen to receive chastisement to be fixed firmly into place, rendering them helpless to the mistress' lash, while the open structure allows a second lady of negotiable virtue, generally younger and prettier, to apply manual stimulation with simultaneous effect.

Birching

A traditional and respected form of corporal punishment frequently corrupted to carnal ends. In essence, the practice involves striking the naked posteriors of the recipient with a bundle of birch twigs, but among aficionados this has been elevated to the status of a ritual.

{Fig. 5} 'It should be noted that there is no practical difference between birching
as administered for punishment and as a form of carnality'

While birching literature tends to consider the practice from a scholastic and lavenderistic perspective its origins are rustic, as a common form of domestic discipline in rural settings, and we shall therefore consider the matter from the perspective of a female recipient. Once persuaded, by whatever means, that she is to receive a birching, the ritual begins.

First, she is sent out into the woods, where she must locate a clump of birch. She must pick twelve bushy twigs of approximately one yard in length, which she must bind into a bundle using a ribbon, traditionally taken from her hair. This binding forms the handle of the birch, which is generally some one third the total length, with the tips of the twigs extending to form the business end.

Returning home, or to wherever she is to be beaten, she must present the birch to her persecutor, who will decide if it is of adequate quality. If the judgement goes against her, her punishment will be increased and she will be sent back into the woods to make a second birch. Extreme sadists have been known to continue this cycle until a dozen or more birches have been collected, which is sufficient to drive even a willing victim into a state of apprehension close to dementia.

The third part of the ritual is dependent on the season. In the spring and early summer, the birch twigs will be supple and may be put to use immediately. However, as the year progresses into late summer and autumn, the twigs harden and therefore need to be soaked in brine. During winter the twigs are at their hardest, and also brittle, so break easily when used. Opinion varies as to whether this is a good or a bad thing, but the true enthusiast will keep a selection of summer-picked birches ready in a tub of brine at all times. It should be noted that brine is an antiseptic and stings when applied to blemished skin, thus augmenting both the hygiene and the efficacy of the punishment process.

Once the birch is ready, the recipient will be taken to a room sufficiently large for her effective chastisement, frequently a barn, although open-air birchings are not uncommon. Here, she will either be obliged to clutch her ankles, or, ideally, be fastened across a custom-made birching horse, such as those produced by Messrs J--- and G----- B---- of Ringwood in Dorset, which also employs a system of straps to ensure immobility. In either case the effect is to bring her bottom into full prominence. Her clothes are then lifted onto her back and her drawers unfastened and let down so as to ensure the complete exposure of her posteriors.

She is then whipped. This is done slowly, to an exact rhythm, and after each stroke she is obliged to cry out how many have been given and to either thank her persecutor for chastising her or apologise for whatever misdemeanour earned her the beating in the first place, sometimes both. On completion of the punishment she must kiss the birch rod and is then sent into the corner to contemplate the indignity of her position as she displays her beaten posteriors.

It should be noted that there is little or no practical difference between birching as administered for punishment and as a form of carnality, save in that the erotic form is generally followed by a lewd act. *See fig. 5*

Borborolagnia

Known to the vulgar as 'mudlarking', this is a corruption of that manly outdoor joy known to every schoolboy whereby playful combat conducted in mud is carried out not to build the character and aid in physical development, but for purposes of carnal indulgence. Futhermore, I regret to say, that those who where supreme sportsmen in their schooldays are all too often the very same ones who carry the depraved form of this practice into adult life.

Thus we have Mr J---- E----, twice Victor Ludorum, captain of cricket and rugby and fencing while at school, who, despite having risen to prominence in the field of politics, made a habit of offering the sum of one guinea to any woman willing to go three rounds of catch-as-catch-can wrestling with him in a ring filled to a depth of one foot with notably glutinous mud. Initially this offer was only extended to his wife and maids, who quickly grew tired of being held down while their chemises and drawers were loaded with mud or removed and their posteriors smacked, but, still a sportsman and so keen for a sterner contest, Mr E---- soon threw the challenge open to all comers. This proved a mistake, as it was accepted by Mrs G------- P----, wife to the local butcher and a woman capable of heaving an entire beef carcass across her shoulders, who beat him so comprehensively that he gave up this vice and took up raffia work in its place.

Bos Eroticus

A form of zoomutatolagnia, or animal transformation fantasy to employ the vulgar term. This is popularly referred to as 'cow-girls', and is discovered occasionally in rural areas and also among lactanolagniacs. Both men and women may be involved, clothing is not worn, a crawling position is adopted and actors' greasepaint is applied to the body, sometimes also a mask or tail, thus providing the subject the approximate appearance of the common cow (*Bos taurus*) or, in the male case, the bull.

Male enthusiasts for this penchant may be broadly divided into two categories, those who keep cow-girls for the purposes of erotic congress and lactanolagniacs. The former group generally share the fetish completely, making themselves up with equal diligence and pursuing their intended mounts around a suitable field until they achieve their goal. This is a display which I personally, while filled with an inevitable distaste for their lewd antics, cannot help but find comic. Lactanolagniacs find a different use for their cow-girls, selecting only ladies of ample personal development in the bosom and utilising them for the supply of milk and other dairy products, a process usually conducted complete with milking stool, pails, churns and other necessities. The cheese is especially good.

The colour given to cow-girls is dependent on region. In Devon, where the cattle are as red as the soil, so the cow-girl is traditionally painted red, as exemplified by the herd of Sir J----- H------ at Kilkampton Manor just north of Exeter. In East

Anglia, where a strong Dutch influence is felt, it is the Friesian breed we see most frequently and likewise the cow-girls of Essex and Suffolk tend to be painted white with patches of black. In Scotland, where the magnificent Aberdeen Angus holds sway, girls are equipped with furry suits and broad horns, both taken from the beasts they are made up to resemble.

I am informed that a fetish of the same name but completely different in character exists in the Americas, wherein young ladies are dressed up in plaid shirts, wide-brimmed hats, boots of tooled leather equipped with spurs, and, most importantly, tight blue trousers designed to exhibit their posterior charms. No doubt this is a most disgraceful display, but it is one I have not yet had the opportunity to witness.

Burlesque

A theatrical display of a comical and vulgar nature, often including humorous dance and even striptease. The concept may be traced back to the ancient Greeks, who appear to have been possessed of an elaborate, if at times improper, sense of amusement. The plays of A-----------, and in particular, *Lysistrata*, so recently the subject of a series of disgraceful illustrations by Mr A----- B--------, may serve as example.

Modern burlesque performances may be divided into two principal categories: vulgar parodies of existing works made to suit the low humour of the intended audience by the inclusion of lewd language and hints of the display of bosoms and posteriors, and performances that focus on the teasing display of bosoms and posteriors purely for their own sake, and which have no redeeming features whatsoever. Thus is art mocked by the male body made ludicrous and the female body flaunted for public crapulence.

My researches have, on occasion, brought me into burlesque theatres, where I have observed corruptions of the works of our greatest playwrights so grotesque in their licentiousness that it borders upon the sacrilegious. For example, a version of Mr W------ S----------'s *A Midsummer Night's Dream* in which Titania was played by a lovely young lady of truly elfin aspect and the palest hair I have ever seen. She did not merely fall in love with Bottom, portrayed by a grotesque buffoon who barely needed to don a mask in order to achieve the part, but removed her garments for him, until she stood stark naked upon the stage for all to see. Furthermore, it is rumoured that when the troupe in question performs in Paris, these two complete a lewd act on stage, an outrage I feel obliged to investigate at the earliest opportunity.

Calcolagnia

The carnal enjoyment of being trodden on or trampled, which, like so much that is deviant, is incomprehensible to the normal mind. Nevertheless, it is a not uncommon practice, with cases recorded from various social strata and at various historical periods. Much the commonest form is for a male calcolagniac to desire being trampled upon by a female, although all possible combinations between the two human sexes are clearly practical and have presumably been indulged in at one time or another.

A male calcolagniac will typically select a partner of slender or even elfin proportions, whom he will invite to walk upon his prostrate form, often while taking carnal gratification of the manual variety. Most often the lady is required to be barefoot, or in her stockinged feet, although some prefer slippers, dainty shoes or even boots, but footwear or the lack of it almost invariably plays an important part in the specifics of the calcolagniac's need. A typical example is provided by Mr A----- U-----------, of Yorkshire, whose choice was for an exceptionally small lady friend to walk on his body in a pair of red silk carpet slippers, which she would then remove to perform what must have been a remarkably dextrous application of her feet to his virile member. She was apparently skilled in the art of Irish dance. At the opposite extreme is the case of the late Colonel R-------- G-----, who, in rainy weather, would send his wife out into the garden in nothing but a pair of regulation army boots, while he would lie naked across the doorway of the scullery so that on her return to the house he might be used as a doormat. Let this be a cautionary tale, as Mrs R-------- G----- was fond of both roasts and puddings, which led, after some years of this practice, to the Colonel's untimely demise.

{Fig. 6} 'Whom he will invite to walk upon his prostrate form'

For the female calcolagniac who desires to be trodden on, practicality will usually intrude in view of her physical delicacy and the typically greater weight of the male, thus obliging her to take up the sapphic habit. Mrs A---- B----, for example, while an undoubted calcolagniac, declined to indulge her habit with her lawfully wedded husband and instead used to visit a retired ballet dancer, Miss S---- G-----, at whose home she was not only trampled on but also whipped across the posteriors with a dried bull's pizzle. When challenged, she claimed this was a medical treatment designed to alleviate stiffness in the musculature. *See fig. 6*

Cane

That most English of devices of chastisement, which, like every single other device of chastisement I have been able to discover, has been pressed into service as an adjunct to the beastly pleasures of carnal flagellation. Indeed, my researches show that the cane is the most popular of all such implements from the Scottish border to Land's End, excepting only Wales, whose flagellant inhabitants appear to have little taste for refinement and prefer to use switches made of twigs or reeds picked from the hedgerows or moorlands. The cane, then, is deserving of full analysis as an instrument of depravity, among which it may reasonably be considered the queen.

First, let us consider type and construction. Three primary types of cane exist, all imported from our Imperial possessions in Burma and the Malay peninsula, and indeed, it is since the inclusion of these lands in our great Empire that the cane has reached its pre-eminent position as an implement of both scholastic and erotic chastisement, replacing the birch. I do not include bamboo, which is fit only for the support of indoor plants in their pots, or garden work. Kooboo is the least of the canes, a flexible, inexpensive rattan of light weight and pale colour which is employed by the great majority of our cane makers for their ordinary stock. Second best in quality is the Mang-Gon, or dragon cane, a darker, denser rattan, heavier in the hand and more reliable in the grip. Best of all is malacca, denser and more rigid still, yet with all the flexibility required for its purpose, while the characteristic nodules render it superior in both appearance and effect.

Having secured a yard rod of one or another of the above canes, it should be soaked in water for a week to render it supple before the upper part is bent into the traditional crook-shaped handle and tied in place. A further week is required for the cane to dry properly, during which time it should be left hanging vertically in warm, dry air, thus ensuring that aside from the handle it remains perfectly straight. Once dry, each tip should be carefully rubbed down with sandpaper and the cane left to stand for a further week in a pot of light oil – Rustock and Baker's Rifle Oil is my personal choice – which the wood will take up to ensure suppleness and preserve your carefully made implement in good condition for a decade or more.

Having taken such care in the production of the implement, even the most depraved and corrupted will wish to take equal care in its use. Indeed, it is the erotic flagellant and not the conventional disciplinarian who has elevated the use of the cane almost to an art. A hundred subtleties exist in the administration of the cane, including informing the recipient of the exact time and place of her punishment hours or even days in advance to ensure that she suffers the greatest possible degree of anticipation; having her go for some while with no drawers beneath her dress, again to heighten her sense of anticipation; making her display herself in an elaborate ritual such as touching her toes while her skirts are thrown one by one onto her back and she is lectured on her supposed misdemeanour; having her lie on her back with her hands gripping her ankles while the punishment is administered, a most indecent position; obliging her to count each stroke as it falls and, should she fail, beginning the process all over again. Such are the multitudinous wiles of the master, or mistress, of the cane. My own researches have led me to become

a skilled practitioner. Indeed, when working on an eager subject, such as Miss
L--- F------, a maidservant addicted to this particular form of erotic chastisement,
I have discovered that it is possible to cause a condition of erotic hysteria with the
cane alone.

Canis Eroticus

Popularly known as 'puppy-play' or 'doggy-girls', this is an animal transformation
fantasy in which the subject behaves as a dog (*Canis familiaris*). Perhaps
curiously, this has little to do with the common phrase 'treated like a dog', which you
might expect to be readily taken up by sadists and their masochistic counterparts.
Rather, puppy-play tends to concentrate on sensual practices, more playful than
cruel, although no less depraved, such as begging, the eating of treats from the
hand, and rolling on the floor so that the master or mistress may tickle the 'puppy's'
tummy.

Even in the most depraved cases there is little cruelty, although few of the
practices listed in this volume exceed that indulged in by Sir J------ and Lady
A---- at their Northamptonshire home for sheer, monstrous outrage to propriety.
Both are enthusiasts for Canis Eroticus, and both are of a dominant and sadistic
nature, making it impractical for them to indulge their beastly desires upon each
other. They therefore choose their servants with care, feigning charity as they
select hopeless nymphomaniacs from refuges for fallen women and allowing
these women in turn to recommend men. This means that they have no difficulty
in conducting what is probably the most depraved game I have ever had the
misfortune to witness. First, a pretty maid is stripped of her ordinary clothes and
puts on in their place a number of peculiar garments made of black sheepskin,
so that her body is covered with a pattern of dense black wool in much the same

manner as one might see on a carefully shaved French poodle, but with her bosom and posteriors quite bare, while ears and a tail with a black woollen pom-pom at the tip are also affixed. Thus attired, she is let loose on the front lawn, as are the butler, Sir J-----'s valet, the chauffeur, both footmen, three gardeners, four groundsmen and the boy who blacks the boots, each attired as a different breed of dog, from the butler as a somewhat elderly mastiff to the boy as a basset hound. They are then entitled to pursue the maid and, on catching her, to take turns with her, in strict order of precedence.

Carpet Beater

An ordinary household implement, which, when applied to the naked posteriors with moderate force produces sharp, tingling sensations. This is notably popular among flagellants of the serving classes, and in particular maids, those employed by Mrs E----- L---- of 47 Nasturtium Villas, Muswell Hill, providing an excellent example of the practice. These girls, who are apparently oblivious to even the most self-evident of moral practices, have been observed in the garden of their residence, not only taking turns to apply a carpet beater to each other's posteriors, but laughing and exchanging jests as they did so, a quite outrageous display that continued for upwards of an hour before being brought to a halt by the housekeeper, who, I greatly hope, thrashed the pair of them with some more efficaceous implement. *See fig. 7*

{Fig. 7} 'These girls, who are apparently oblivious to even the most self-evident of moral practices'

Cattus Eroticus

Generally know as 'pussy-play' or 'pussy-girls', in which the participants take on the characteristics of the domestic cat (*Felis domesticus*) for purposes of carnal enjoyment.

As with most examples of animal transformation fantasy, it is the female who most frequently desires to be the cat, but, unusually, she has little need for a male counterpart, let alone a master or mistress. Rather, like the animal she seeks to imitate, the pussy-girl is an independent creature, perhaps permitting a man or woman to stroke her, tickle her under her chin or feed her delicacies, but reacting to liberties with spitting and vicious swipes of her claws. Nevertheless, let there be no mistaking the carnal nature of this habit, for the pussy-girl is a confirmed onanist, and will often spend many hours in self-indulgence before bringing herself to a state of erotic hysteria.

Nor should this be regarded as a masochistic or submissive habit, as demonstrated by Miss E--------- P------, who produced for herself a tight-fitting suit of black velvet complete with ears, whiskers, a tail and curved steel claws sewn into gloves reinforced with leather. Thus attired, she would attend those depraved parties thrown by the notorious Disciples of Eros, where she was invariably among the most beautiful and alluring of women, but also highly dangerous, by reason of encouraging men to mount her by rolling on her back, rubbing her neck against their legs and lifting her exceedingly pert posterior so as to invite entry, all in the manner of a female cat, only to allow merely the briefest of insertions before twisting about and striking out with her claws. *See fig. 8*

{Fig. 8} 'An independent creature, perhaps permitting a man or woman to stroke her, tickle her under her chin or feed her delicacies, but reacting to liberties with spitting and vicious swipes of her claws'

Cephalopodophilia

A most curious paraphilia probably originating in the Japanese archipelago and almost certainly restricted to the fevered imaginations of a few extraordinarily depraved individuals. Nevertheless, it forms a remarkably common motif in the artwork of those islands and might just conceivably be based on reality.

The most noted exponent of this practice was the artist H------, whose remarkable work entitled *The Dream of the Fisherman's Wife* shows a woman entwined in the tentacles of not one, but two octopi (*Octopus hongkongensis*), a large and a small. My first thought on seeing this was that it represented some ghastly nightmare, but on closer inspection the larger of the two octopi is clearly performing an act of kolpolagnia, in which the woman seems to be taking a great deal of pleasure. The precise nature of the interaction between the woman and the smaller octopus is not so easy to elucidate. She appears to be sucking its nose, but as the octopus possesses no such organ this is evidently a false impression, while as the octopus reproduces by means of a specialised tentacle, the hectocotyle, if she is supposed to be indulging in irrumation then either she, or the artist, is in error.

I have been to Japan only once, and that briefly, as one of the many Europeans invited by that country to teach on diverse matters, although I found that the food did not suit me and quickly returned. During that period I saw this peculiar picture reproduced several times, as well as others on the same theme and again as 'netsuke', in this last case involving not only octopus but squid. Netsuke are exquisitely carved ornaments worn as an element of formal dress, but are often extraordinarily depraved, being carved to depict every sort of beastliness. This is all the more remarkable, because while I do not claim to understand Japanese social mores, and they are of course heathens, they seem in general a most courteous people. How then to explain a habit which in our own islands would be the equivalent of attending a respectable dinner party in immaculate dress save for pinning one's cravat with a carved representation of a buxom housemaid having her posteriors smacked?

Chastity

It may seem strange to find a virtue among the vices, but even chastity can be corrupted. Indeed, I am grieved to report that those devices manufactured for the enforcement of chastity, for men and women alike, enjoy far healthier sales among the depraved than they do among the virtuous.

Take, for example, Messrs N----- and K---'s Protective Girdle, an entirely innocent device designed to be worn by maidens when travelling abroad, or when in the company of potentially ardent young men but the absence of a suitable chaperone. These, so I am informed, are bitterly resented by the haughty young women of today and very few indeed are sold for their proper purpose. By contrast, some three a week are purchased for use in bordellos, with customers as far afield as India, Spain and the Hebridean Islands. One notorious London rake, Sir T----- C-----, maintains a standing order so that he may ensure that his numerous mistresses remain in eager fettle for his visits.

Male chastity is also widely practised among the debauched, generally as an element of submission to the will of a cruel or flagellant Mistress. Again, considerable irony exists, for those devices originally designed by the eminent American nutritionist Mr J--- H----- K------ to guard against onanism are frequently employed for purposes almost diametrically opposed to that prescribed by the manufacturer. Mr W------ W------, for example, employs the services of Madame V----- to hold the key to such a device, releasing him only once a fortnight on payment of a not inconsiderable fee and locking him up once again as soon as their business is concluded. Chastity, in Mr W------ W--'----s case, can clearly not be defined as a virtue.

Chausophilia

The association of carnal desire with close-fitting leg wear, and in particular sheer silk stockings as worn by women of at least moderate wealth or social rank. So far as I have been able to determine, it is an exclusively male form of depravity, although as women wear stockings as a matter of course it may simply be that they are better able to conceal their penchant. Among men I have identified three primary groups, although there is considerable overlap: those who enjoy stockings on a lady, those who enjoy wearing stockings themselves, and those who enjoy stockings as stockings.

This last mentioned might be regarded as the purest form of Chausophilia, in that it is the object itself which has become the focus of devotion. Such a man is a low fellow, in carnal habit a specialised onanist given to the grotesque abuse of that very article of clothing he worships. His habits inevitably mean he gets through great numbers of stockings, and he is therefore often to be found in the relevant departments of the nation's emporia, lurking guiltily in the background as he attempts to pluck up the courage to make a purchase.

Men may dress in stockings for a variety of reasons, more or less beastly, but the chausophile is not necessarily otherwise a transvestite and derives a specific pleasure from the wearing of stockings. Many is the gentleman of the city or politician who goes to work with a pair of smooth, silken lady's stockings beneath his trousers and no one the wiser save possibly his wife or mistress.

More prevalent by far is the desire to enjoy a lady in stockings, although it must be said with regret that to a chausophile the lady herself comes a poor second to her stockings, or indeed third, after her legs, which he tends to regard much as a horticulturist might regard a pot, essential for the support of that which he considers true beauty. Thus matters proceed, and the lady who finds herself entrapped by a chausophile must be prepared to spend many hours with her skirts and petticoats hitched up, perhaps even without her drawers, while he traces his fingers lovingly over the sheer silk encasing her legs.

Furthermore, in this we have one of the most elaborate of all forms of beastliness, so much so that it often becomes sheer pedantry. Each practitioner, I have found, will have strong individual tastes, which he tends to regard as absolute, and all alternatives as utterly unacceptable, an attitude to which some bring an almost religious fervour. Such points include colour, length, the way the seam is formed, whether and how the toe and heel are reinforced, the weight of silk in which the stocking should be made (there are even those who prefer wool or linen) and a dozen other lesser factors, without even considering the debate between the old fashioned garter and that peculiarly French contrivance designed by Mr G------ E-----, the suspender.

A large book might very easily be written on this subject, but the definitive illustration is provided by the case of Sir R----- M-------- and Lord N------, who fought a duel over the issue of whether the reinforced heel piece of a lady's stocking should be of a diamond or oval shape. This encounter took place on Primrose Hill after a night of drunken excess in a house of ill repute at nearby St John's Wood, with each of the duellists amply supported by fellows of like mind and ladies of easy virtue, these last *en déshabillé* so that they might display those undergarments which had led to the altercation. Bordellos, it seems, are not well stocked with either pistols or swords, and the antagonists therefore fought with riding whips, which they had no difficulty in obtaining, and used chamberpots as shields. Nor was this a bloodless matter, but fought with such ferocity that had it not been for the timely intervention of the Metropolitan Police one man or the other would almost certainly have been carried dead from the field.

Chionolagnia

The association of carnal pleasure with snow. This is a rare form of beastliness, and unusual in that it is associated almost exclusively with the female, although I suspect that this is due to the marked shrinkage of the virile member upon exposure to the cold rather than any innate difference between the genders.

An interesting example is provided by the Dowager Duchess of S---------, a sadistic chionolagniac who used to send her young wards out onto the moors of her native Scotland in nothing but their underwear and with their drawers stuffed with snow. Her claim was that this process ensured robust health and strength of character in her charges, but I suspect otherwise. For one thing it was her invariable practice to spank all three girls afterwards, ostensibly to restore the circulation to their chilled posteriors, and for another all four slept in the same enormous bed, this despite occupying a castle of over seventy rooms. This practice she excused on the grounds of household economy.

Chirolagnia

Manual stimulation of the private parts by another person, either male or female, lavenderistic or sapphic. While lewd, this practice is perhaps not entirely inexcusable between man and wife, so long as it is conducted in a suitably reserved manner and in the matrimonial bed. I am also inclined to take an attitude of Christian forbearance to another common use of this technique, which is for young ladies to employ it in order to deflect amorous suitors from attempting yet more intimate intrusions. However, I will not excuse the altogether too common and entirely unnecessary practice of unfastening their upper clothing while doing so, and in any event such dispensations must come with a cautionary tale.

When Miss F------ J---- first went into service as a scullery maid she found herself
the object of attention of the various tradesmen and errand boys who would call
at the kitchen door of the comfortable detached villa in which she was employed.
Given her abundant charms this was hardly surprising, but she is a modest girl and
was suitably flattered. It was the butcher's boy who first declared his love for her,
and with such outpourings of desire and earnest longing that she first allowed him
to kiss her and then, after listening to a long and ardent speech, promised to assuage
his need by taking him in her hand. This she duly did, among the raspberry canes in
the kitchen garden.

After a couple of turns he managed to persuade her that it was accepted practice
for girls to perform this act with their bosoms naked, which display became part
of their routine, each Tuesday and Thursday. She was a little surprised when the
fishmonger began to pay court to her, as he was not only an elderly and corpulent
fellow but married, and yet in her generosity of spirit she acceded to his lewd
request, performed in the larder each Friday. A month passed and she had added
the grocer's boy to her list of lovers, accommodated on Mondays and Wednesdays
among the runner beans in one corner of the vegetable patch, along with the knife
grinder, on Saturdays in the coal cellar, and, I very much regret to say, a local
curate, who would walk her home from church on Sundays and have her discharge
him behind the stables. It was only when similar demands began to come from
the paper boy and the baker, both of whom called daily, that she began to feel put
upon, but so large hearted is she that she steeled herself to the task, taking it on
both wherever and whenever the opportunity presented itself.

All this came to light only when the cook noticed that Miss F------ J---- suffered
from constantly sore wrists, but the tradesmen, who were in cahoots, presented
a united front and denied everything. The unfortunate girl was then accused of
lying and of obsessive onanism, leading to her dismissal, without references. Her
subsequent travails were extensive, and her mild and accepting nature frequently
taken advantage of, but I am pleased to say she is now safely in my employ.

Cinematograph

On the evening of the twenty-eighth of December, 1895, the brothers L------ gave a demonstration of this remarkable invention in the Salon Indien of the Grand Café at 4, Boulevard des Capucines, Paris. On the evening of the twenty-ninth of December, 1895, the brothers G------ gave a demonstration of a near identical contrivance in the Salon Remédial of their sister's house of ill repute at 6, Rue St Martin, Paris. The principal distinction between the two events was that while the brothers L------ showed a series of respectable episodes from life in and around the cities of Lyon and Marseille, the brothers G------ showed Mlle F--- G------ in the process of disrobing for her bath.

Thus is illustrated the extraordinary vigour and industry which the pornographer applies to his trade, to say nothing of the depravity inherent in the French as a race. However, it must not be supposed that the brothers G------ managed to replicate the invention of the brothers L------ in a single day. Had the Salon Remédial not been required for its usual purposes the previous evening, the brothers G------ might even have given their disgraceful performance in advance of their rivals. In the November of the same year a German, one Herr M--- S-----------, had demonstrated a similar device at the Wintergarten, while the concept of projecting moving pictures dates back to the 'seventies if not earlier. Nor were the brothers G------ the first to abuse such inventions, as my own collection contains a zoopraxiscope disc showing a lewd dance in silhouette, made by some unknown pornographer of the early 'eighties.

What is evident is that no sooner does man create some new and useful tool for the furtherance of civilisation than it will be put to improper use, and in no case is this more true than that of the cinematograph. In the five short years since the brothers L------ gave their demonstration, cinematography has spread across the world, and will undoubtedly become an important tool for both entertainment and education. However, by my own estimate, for every interesting or educational cinematograph produced at least two lewd ones come into being.

Paris is the centre of this licentious trade, and at 6, Rue St Martin the entire basement has now been converted into a cinematograph theatre specifically for the demonstration of their outrageous productions. This enterprise now brings in almost as much income as the remainder of what is one of the busiest and most prestigious houses of ill repute in the city, to say nothing of the effect it has on the patrons and therefore trade. Although the authorities in our own country would never tolerate such abuses, the cinematographs of the brothers G------ and others have frequently been shown at the gatherings of those societies dedicated to debauchery, while rumour has it that a cellar somewhere in Clerkenwell is regularly made available for more public performances.

As an incidental note to this entry, I feel it incumbent upon myself to point out that my appearance in *Douche après le Bain de Mademoiselle Fifi-Armelle* (1897) was not voluntary but forced upon me by the necessity of maintaining the pretence of patronage at 6, Rue St Martin in order that I might properly conduct my researches. Also, the gentleman in the leather mask who appears briefly in *Les Laveuses Attrapées* (1897) is not me, despite a degree of physical similarity, nor is the clysopomp operator in *Les Laveuses Attrapées pour la Vingtième Fois* (1899), while the man in the green silk dress and golden leather boots in *La Tante et le Mouflon* (1900) has nothing to do with me whatsoever.

Cohibeolagnia

The general practice of restricting movement, most frequently by systems of bondage or with fetters, but also, on occasion, by enclosure within a cage or by the application of some such device as Dr M-------'s patent finger trap, which allows the digits to be inserted but not withdrawn.

Restraint may also be applied by the simple device of holding somebody down, a practice popular among flagellants. Sir L----- H------, for instance, adds to the enjoyment of birching his paramours and maids by having the head groom horse the girl up on his back, holding her by her wrists with her feet dangling clear of the ground. Thus displayed, her posteriors may be exposed and thrashed at leisure, also fondled, tickled and generally molested in any manner that takes his fancy, which represents the essence of erotic restraint.

Collaring

A popular device among those depraved and secretive societies which have for long been a blot on the escutcheon of our more elevated classes, collaring describes a ritual whereby one individual confirms herself, or more rarely himself, as the erotic slave of another, or more frequently of a group. Of the seventeen distinct societies of this type of which I am aware, fourteen use collaring rituals of one sort or another, and each of these fourteen is unique. The only unifying factor is that a collar is affixed around the neck of the enslaved.

The Disciples of Eros, for example, use beautifully crafted collars of woven silver filigree, so delicate and of such artistry that they may be worn in public and pass without adverse comment from the uninitiated. They are, however, fastened by a discreet weld and quite impossible to remove save with strong tools, so that whatever others may think, she who has been proclaimed the property of the society is never for a moment in doubt as to her status. These collars are applied in a ritual I have been privileged to witness, and which, despite its depraved nature, carries a certain beauty. Each disciple, clad in hooded robes of crimson silk, carries a large candle, illuminating the circle in which they stand. The girl who is due to be collared is led forward by two of her sisters in shame and vice, they being naked while she wears a simple cotton shift. As she reaches the official who is to perform the ceremony her shift is removed and she falls to a kneeling position, now quite naked, bowing her head in front of the man she has chosen to become her master. The collar is applied to the sound of low, sonorous chanting, and sealed in place, which is the signal for the wine and cheese to be brought out and for the assembly to descend into orgiastic extravagance.

Companion

A generally blameless profession which young ladies should nevertheless approach with care, ensuring that their prospective employer is above reproach prior to commencing employment. I say this advisedly, and in the light of several regrettable instances in which companions have found themselves taken advantage of in unexpected ways.

It is in the nature of the post that a companion will find herself entirely dependent on her employer, often far from home, and if in foreign lands frequently unable to speak the local tongue. In normal circumstances these considerations are of no particular consequence, but in rare, abnormal circumstances a young lady may find herself compromised, helpless to prevent her own seduction or even lured into beastliness by the very person she relies upon for protection. I shall cite two examples.

Miss L------ M------- was a young lady from an impoverished but respectable family of Kincardineshire in Scotland, and as such typical of the class who tend to adopt this profession. So careful had been her upbringing, and so absolute the Christian rule of her parents, that she possessed a beautiful innocence, with no knowledge whatsoever of the carnal sins of humanity and the misuse to which the human body can be put. Upon reaching her majority, she was accepted into the employment of the Earl of S---------, that she might act in the capacity of lady's companion to his eldest daughter, Lady K------. The winter nights are long in the north of Scotland, and the climate distinctly unfavourable, so Miss M------- thought Lady K------'s suggestion that they share a bed no more than common sense and a wise economy. How she regarded Lady K------'s subsequent behaviour I cannot be certain, but I am inclined to be charitable and put her acquiescence down to extreme innocence. She probably thought that having her posteriors gently smacked before bed as punishment in anticipation of sin was a common practice in the Highlands. Presumably she felt that as a conscientious employee she should do as she was told, and therefore accepted Lady K------'s habit of riding her around the room in the nude as a simple eccentricity. Possibly she even regarded being told to go down the bed and perform a lewd act with her tongue as a reasonable request from her Mistress. What is certain is that in five short years she changed from a veritable icon of innocence and chastity to one of the lewdest and least reserved sapphists I have ever encountered.

An equally salutary example is provided by the story of Miss R------ M---, who gained a post as companion to somebody calling herself Mrs D------- through a firm specialising in the hire of servants. Mrs D------- was a large woman, of middle age and apparent respectability, at least while in England. A trip to the spa town of Baden Baden in southern Germany was arranged, and as they travelled Miss M--- became increasingly concerned at the quality of her employer's attention when she disrobed for bed. Only in Neustadt an der Weinstrause did she discover the awful truth, that Mrs D------- was in fact a man, one Mr G----- S----, who had set out to seduce her from the start. By then it was too late, for she had allowed him to peruse every intimate detail of her body and had little choice but to surrender to his machinations. Having had his wicked way, he abandoned her, and it was only by good fortune that I happened to be conducting my researches in the area at the time, realised that she was English due to her poor grasp of instructions given in German, and was able to return her to her home. Mr G----- S---- I horsewhipped on the steps of his club, the West London Philatelists Association, in Bayswater.

Corsetry Fetishism

No item of female apparel has managed to escape the attention of fetishists, but some have attracted more than others and prominent among these is the corset. As the garment is designed not for practical purposes but in order to enhance the contours of a lady's figure, it is unsurprising that those of a lewd nature, both male and female, should be attracted to it, for, regrettable as it may be, that is their nature.

The background of corsetry is too large a subject to consider here, save to say that their purpose is to enhance the waist by reducing it to the minimum feasible circumference, and thus to enhance the posteriors and bosom by comparison, while also providing support for the latter. These facts alone are considered scandalous by many of our stricter religious groupings, who believe, and rightly so, that it is both improper to make such a display of a lady's physical attributes and ungodly to seek to enhance what the Lord has seen fit to provide. Couturiers, and particularly corsetiers, although not otherwise a particularly irreligious group, plainly disagree, as, it seems, do the vast majority of the ladies themselves. Thus, as of the present date, the great majority of women who can afford them wear corsets, as do a minority of men.

With a few minor exceptions, corsetry fetishism may be divided into two distinct yet mutually reinforcing categories, that of women who receive carnal enjoyment from the wearing of corsets and that of men who receive carnal enjoyment from associating with women in corsets. The rare corset-obsessed lavenderist need not concern us unduly in this instance.

What then motivates the lady who corsets herself not for reasons of fashion or the pleasure of others, but for the sake of the process itself? At the simplest level there is the matter of self adornment, a common vanity, and one which need not necessarily involve others at all. Thus, while one might expect such an intimate garment to be plain and functional in design, this is by no means always the case. Even quite respectable maiden ladies, those who would never dream of allowing themselves to be observed *en déshabillé* by a gentleman, display a marked preference for corsets made of rich fabric, coloured and adorned to the extent permitted by their purse. The Dowager Duchess of D-----, for instance, a lady who has been widowed these twenty-two years and would not dream of undressing in the presence of another save her maid, wears a magnificent corset panelled in lilac satin and embroidered with exotic butterflies. Any doubt that there might be as to the erotic nature of her choice must be dispelled by the fact that she invariably retains her corset while indulging certain sapphic practices with the maid in question.

Rarer, but somewhat easier to assess, is the pleasure taken in the restrictive feelings provided by the corset and the consequential prominence of the bosom and posteriors. The case of Miss A-------- H---- provides ample illustration. This lady, on undressing, habitually removes everything but her corset and stockings, then moves to a tall mirror on the door of her wardrobe. Watching her reflection, she will move her hands gently over her body, tracing the contours of her waist within her corset, which provides a measurement I estimate as no more than twenty inches. She will also touch the laces and anterior fastenings of her corset, turning about as she does so in order that she may admire her side and rear aspects. Gradually, her explorations of her body grow bolder, her fingers lingering on the swell of her bosom, hips and posterior charms, until with a sudden exclamation she will lose all control and bring herself to a peak of erotic hysteria. Never have I observed her do this without one or another of her extensive collection of corsets on and laced as tight as it will go.

Any gentleman who chanced to observe Miss A-------- H----, save those of the utmost rectitude, might find himself with amorous intentions, but that would not make him a corset fetishist. The true fetishist must, by definition, give preference not to the lady herself, however exquisite her beauty, but to the object of his devotions, be it animate or not. Thus we have Sir G------ R-----, who has lined the upper passage of his private mansion with exquisitely crafted female mannequins, full at bosom and at hip, and each and every one clad in a beautiful corset which he, in person, has removed from its original owner following her seduction and a bout of erotic congress.

Cosmetic Indulgence

A practice so prevalent both geographically and historically that to denounce it from the pulpit is to invite ridicule, and yet it is without doubt thoroughly beastly. Consider the Phœnicians, who openly admitted that the purpose of women reddening their lips was to mimic the private parts, and in particular to invite irrumation. They were at least honest, while in our own culture this depraved habit is not only commonplace, but prevalent at every level of society. The same is true of the colouring of the cheeks, a well known symptom of carnal arousal, and also the painting of the eyes to make them appear large and languid. What greater outrage could there be than for women to wander the streets as if in immediate anticipation of erotic congress, and yet this beastly habit is presented as simple, harmless adornment. This may be through innocence, but I suspect it is more often through deliberate falsehood, thus heaping scandal upon scandal.

So general has this habit become, that it is not always easy to distinguish the lady who at least considers herself virtuous from her openly lewd sisters, thus leading to frequent and embarrassing misunderstandings for not only gentlemen of beastly intent, but those who wish either to save the girl in question from sin or to conduct serious research.

Dance

An instrument of beastliness posing as innocent entertainment.

It is true that prior to the Napoleonic wars dance was, at least among persons of quality, a reserved and civil affair, equipped with an elaborate etiquette to ensure that the bounds of propriety were never exceeded. Sadly, matters began to decay with the introduction of the waltz and have been in decline ever since. Gone are the stately cotillion and the lively but proper quadrille, to be replaced by dances in which partners clasp each other with an intimacy otherwise unthinkable in company, gyrate in the most undignified manner and in extreme examples even adopt lewd poses. We have the Cakewalk, the Mazurka, the Racket and the Redowa, all of which, I scarcely need point out, have been imported from foreign climes. Worse still is the Tango, a dance born of the hot-blooded Hispanic race, which involves the most extraordinary posturing and displays of human passion arguably improper even within the confines of the matrimonial chamber. All of this is performed in public, under the guise of entertainment, and seen as no worse than trifling and a little silly even by high ecclesiastical authorities.

Also, those people, and especially young ladies, who are conscientiously opposed to dancing are no longer seen as virtuous and sensible, as they were in my youth, but as dull. Thus is foolishness, triviality and licentious behaviour exalted at the expense of those reserved virtues which should be the pride of every Englishwoman, to the general detriment of society and our island race.

Moreover, the polite etiquette of the dance has been seized upon by rakes and lechers in order that they may further their foul intentions. No young lady can refuse the invitation of a gentleman to dance, for she would be guilty of an incivility, and so must accept the advances of the most odious of roués, the least principled of seducers. Her firm young body will be held to his as they disport themselves upon the floor, with her bosom heaving against his chest and his hand most probably

{Fig. 9} 'Who would joyfully remove those few scanty garments they
wore in the daytime and dance naked in the firelight'

placed so low that he is able to cup one rounded posterior in a clammy hand, and from these attentions she has no escape!

Furthermore, much precautionary etiquette has been abandoned altogether. In my day married or young ladies could not leave a ballroom alone under any circumstances, but would be accompanied by some suitable chaperone. Nowadays, even the most delicate flowers of the highest families may be seen slipping out into the darkness for a breath of fresh air or perhaps going upstairs to adjust their toilet, and thus exposing themselves as prey to any wolf who might happen to be lurking in garden or boudoir. Nor do I necessarily refer to such improprietous establishments as the notorious Cremorne Gardens, now thankfully closed, but also to the houses of the great and the good. It is truly monstrous.

I personally do not dance, considering it a foolish and ungodly occupation at best, while in any event I have never been able to properly accomplish the complicated physical evolutions necessary in order to master the art and thus avoid ridicule. However, I have observed dances on many occasions, and my statements on the matter do not come from ignorance. Thus, in final proof of the inherently sordid nature of the entire subject, I am able to reveal that to which all dances and matters of dance tend, open depravity. I refer to dancing for the purposes of blatant erotic display.

The most outrageous examples of this I have observed in far-flung parts of the Empire, as one might expect, where it is by no means unusual for some dusky, heathen maiden to entertain her fellows with the most extraordinary gyrations, often performed in no more than a few scraps of gauze, with bosom and legs naked, or in the most extreme cases, stark naked. Those who doubt my assertions need merely visit the village of Sushamakanga, some two hundred miles inland from Zanzibar. Here, during my time as a missionary, I observed the most beautiful of girls, with skin the colour of polished mahogany, full, smiling lips and great brown eyes that invited lewdness with a glance, who would joyfully remove those few scanty garments they wore in the daytime and dance naked in the firelight. Once their healthy young bodies were glossy with perspiration and their impressive bosoms and fulsome posteriors heaving with exertion, they would come close to some favoured male, who would then be led off into the darkness for carnal indulgence that lacked all inhibition. Nor was this a rare event, but nightly entertainment, and you may be assured that each morning I prayed long and hard for the souls of these unfortunate girls, and for my own.

One might imagine such behaviour unthinkable to the Christian conscience, but I very much regret to say that a visitor to Paris can see displays almost as lewd in any number of houses of ill repute, theatres and low bars. Here, the current fad is for a dance called the cancan. This is, so I am informed, an evolution of the quadrille, although how this lively but essentially chaste dance has come to be corrupted to such an extent I cannot imagine. One or more girls, and I have observed as many as thirty in a line, dance on stage, kicking up their heavily flounced skirts to display shoes, stockings and yet more intimate garments, but the true outrage is in the climax. Moving as one, the girls turn their backs upon the audience, push out their posteriors in imitation of the manner in which a trollop offers herself for erotic congress and flip up their skirts and petticoats to show off the seats of their drawers. In less salubrious establishments this dance is more outrageous still. At the establishment of Madame F--- P----, 56, Rue Fontaine, Paris, for example, the girls perform the dance naked beneath their skirts, while on one particularly drunken night in an estaminet in Boulogne, the name of which I forget, the line of six girls finished by suddenly pulling their drawers wide behind, thus displaying their charms in full and exact detail and providing a shock that caused me to fall from my chair. The girls then joined the audience and so in practice, the only difference between them and my heathen maidens is that while the girls in the estaminet charged five francs for their services, those of Sushamakanga came free. *See fig. 9*

Dechætophilia

The removal of hair by shaving, when associated with the carnal appetites, for whatever reason; a complex paraphilia with several subdivisions which show only limited interrelation. All are rare, and therefore warrant only cursory remarks and a single, peculiar example.

At the simplest level we find the male dechætophiliac who enjoys the sensation of smooth, female skin, be it purely as an æsthetic choice or for some more or less sinister reason. His female counterpart is rarer still, and most likely of the sapphic persuasion, while a relatively high proportion of lavenderists share this vice. Next we have those who take carnal enjoyment in the physical act of shaving themselves and the resultant sensations, both male and female, a solitary pursuit designed primarily as a precursor to onanistic experience. Fewer still take their pleasure in shaving others, and even here this is generally a mild vice, save in rare cases.

Such a case was that of the notorious Barber of Brandenburg, a German lavenderist who took his pleasure in accosting the hirsute in their chambers and shaving both their faces and the hair of their heads before performing an immoral act in the general vicinity.

Discipline

An inevitable and necessary feature of civilisation which is particularly susceptible for corruption to carnal ends. So far as I am aware, every single form of chastisement invented for the purposes of maintaining proper behaviour in the home or law and order in the population at large, save only those of the most

{Fig. 10} 'At the domicile of Mr and Mrs L----- P-----, near Moretonhampstead in Devon, a certain ritual is carried out each Friday evening'

severe nature, has, at some time, been utilised by those of depraved character for the enhancement of their beastly lusts. The simple, homely practice of spanking has, in particular, suffered this fate, to such an extent that I estimate that for every seven sets of posteriors exposed and smacked for the correct and necessary imposition of domestic discipline, two sets are exposed and smacked for the purposes of carnal indulgence. Nor is this simply an excuse for the lascivious male to expose a pair of female nether cheeks, for I have recorded instances between men, between women, and of women spanking men, in the vast majority of which cases both participants have taken pleasure in their lewd and improper conduct.

Thus is discipline made a mockery, and in some households this is carried to an extent at which proper discipline and the erotic form become indistinguishable. At the domicile of Mr and Mrs L----- P-----, near Moretonhampstead in Devon, a certain ritual is carried out each Friday evening, whereby Mr P-----, on receipt of his wages, rides to the White Horse Inn and becomes so beastly drunk that his fellow bibbers have to tie him to his horse in order that he may return home. On arrival he is soundly thrashed by his wife, a woman of monstrous proportions, following which they retire to bed and much stimulated congress.

Specific forms of discipline, and their corruption, are dealt with separately. *See fig. 10*

Domination

T he reverse of, or counterpoint to, submission, and the more easily understandable of the two. It is in the nature of man to wish to conquer nature and win control of his circumstances, and thus perhaps no great surprise that many, particularly men, should seek to extend this practice to the bedchamber. What is perhaps more surprising is that the desire for erotic dominance should be as common among women as it is among men.

{Fig. 11} 'Lord M-----, a man who, while a peer of the realm and lord of seventy thousand acres and an immense forture, also happens to be four feet and eight inches in height'

Indeed, my researches have uncovered an inverse correlation between those characteristics which one associates with the dominant members of our society and their erotic preferences. Thus it is not the largest, nor the most forceful, the most wealthy and the most privileged of birth whom one finds preferring to wield the whip, although there are numerous exceptions, but more often those of small size, lack of will, modest means or low birth. My statistics show that seventy-four per hundred of those who prefer to take a dominant role when engaging in beastly practices possess one or more characteristics which one might ordinarily expect to be associated with a mild or humble nature.

Thus we have Lord M-----, a man who, while a peer of the realm and lord of seventy thousand acres and an immense fortune, also happens to be four feet and eight inches in height. Nevertheless, he is in the habit of flagellating his female staff with extraordinary frequency, and, having concluded their chastisement, of mounting them from the rear, for which purpose he employs a small chair.

A similar case was that of the Baroness B------, who measured only four feet and three inches, but managed to terrorise the greater part of Lower Silesia for a period of nearly three decades during the fourteenth century. Her height, incidentally, I estimate from the size of her crypt and surviving illustrations. If there is any doubt about the tales of erotic flagellation and vampirism associated with her name it must be dispelled by the fact that she was buried with a leather whip, or knout, binding her shroud and a wooden stake through her heart.

At a more mundane level, we find that the average height among madames of flagellant houses in London between 1867 and 1889 was one and a half inches below that of the general female population. In the case of members of those societies given over to wicked practices involving the erotic submission of women the figure is two and one quarter inches for men and precisely two inches for women.

My conclusion then, is that the desire to dominate in an erotic context often stems from feelings of inferiority brought about by inadequate personal characteristics, while the twenty-six per hundred to which this does not apply are presumably merely combining a desire to control their fellow human beings with a depraved attitude to the bedchamber. *See fig. 11*

Dungeon

A construction as old as the stonemason's art, whereby a subterranean chamber with a stout door is set aside for the confinement and castigation of enemies and malefactors, or, in this case, for the furtherance of depravity.

No doubt the less virtuous of our forebears occasionally took advantage of their dungeons for the indulgence of lustful practice upon helpless female captives, but I suspect that even at the height of the mediæval age fewer dungeons existed within the boundaries of the British Isles than do at this present day. For this we must blame, in part at least and freely admitting that there was no malice of intent, Sir W----- S---- and the romantic movement. It was they who were responsible for the revival of heraldry, of mediæval sports such as jousting and tennis, of the ideal of courtly love, and just as surely, of the dungeon.

Thus, while the original dungeon is almost unknown beyond those which survive in scattered castles, newly built dungeons exist between, to my certain knowledge, Wick in the most northerly part of Scotland, and St Just in Cornwall. Almost without exception these are presented as romantic follies, but in all too many cases a single glance from an expert eye reveals that they also serve a more sinister purpose. Thus, for example, we have that dungeon built by Sir J--- M----, who made his fortune in the grocery trade, and on his retirement built an impressive folly overlooking the River Wensley in Yorkshire. For a modest sum one may be shown around this remarkable edifice, including the dungeon, which is amply supplied with racks, pillories, cages and other devices commonly associated with the very worst kind of depravity, and also the largest selection of whips, straps, canes and paddles I have seen outside my own reference collection, as well as sufficient shackles, chains and ropes to restrain at least a score of victims simultaneously. True, he has also a number of devices too horrid to be of use to the eroticist, but these show no signs of use, whereas to judge by the wear and tear on the large pillory with the brass fittings he displays as his centrepiece it is in use on a regular basis. His shackles are also padded, a sure sign of depravity.

E

Ecclesiophilia

An utterly debased practice whereby persons of lewd and ungodly character make deliberate use of church premises for fornication, and from which neither the fear of God nor having a cane applied to their posteriors appears to deter them.

The parish of which I am privileged to hold the living is not particularly well populated, nor, I trust, are the members of my flock notably more depraved than any others. Nevertheless, over the years I have disturbed the youth of the village abusing the hallowed sanctity of my church on no less than forty-seven occasions, including, in the case of R----- S----- and Miss S---- J-------, full erotic congress with the little strumpet bent over the font. They do it to provoke me, I am convinced of it, and the next time I catch them neither one will be able to sit down for a week.

Ecdysiasm

Commonly but expressively known as 'striptease', this involves the removal of clothing in order to excite carnal desire, but done in a gradual or hesitant fashion so as to heighten the sense of anticipation of the observer. With few exceptions the person removing the clothes is female, and the majority of cases the observer, or observers, are male.

Perhaps unsurprisingly, the French attempt to lay claim to this singularly lewd art, citing that the first public striptease took place in Paris on the ninth of February, 1893, when an artist's model named M--- removed her clothes for the edification of the assembled students, apparently while standing on a table to ensure that her audience enjoyed a good view. The police intervened, causing a riot of minor proportions, if only by Parisian standards, and thus ensuring that the event became a scandal. The infamous Moulin Rouge took note of this and the striptease was born.

This is plainly nonsense. I myself have observed ebullient young women remove their clothes for the amusement of an audience, and frequently in a teasing manner, at locations as widely separated as Port Said, San Francisco and Basingstoke in Hampshire, and all of these prior to the date in question. Nor do I claim any of these events to have been original, but suspect that the first such affair took place shortly after women first donned clothes that might then be removed. The earliest recorded instances come from ancient Sumeria, where striptease appears to have taken on a ritual or even religious significance, relating to the removal of clothing and jewellery by the Goddess Inanna in order that she might pass through the seven gates of Hell and so return to ensure the fecundity of the earth in the coming season.

What is not in doubt, however, is that in recent years the French have made the act their own, with officially sanctioned performances up and down the country, from Calais to Cannes and from Biarritz to Belfort, while Paris is now as much the capital of striptease as it is of that most decadent of countries. In the course of my researches I have found myself obliged to visit a great many of these events, and have made notes sufficient to warrant a specialist study of not insubstantial length, but for the present I shall restrict myself to a selection of illustrative case studies.

The emphasis of striptease is not on nudity itself, but on the act of exposure, so that the display of each area of flesh is of the greatest possible significance and thus most highly arousing to the observer. A good illustration of this principle is provided by Mlle F--- l- G---------, whose performance I attended in the city of Verdun, known for its stern fortresses built in defiance of the rapacious Hun. Rather than appear in the flounces and feathers typical of her trade, Mlle F--- came on stage dressed in the uniform of an army nurse, correct in every particular, and which she proceeded to remove to the strains of *La Marseillaise*, item by item, beginning with her white leather gloves and culminating with a pair of smart white drawers fringed only with the one inch of lace trim permitted by regulation, thus successfully whipping her largely military audience into what can only be described as a ferment of erotic patriotism. She was much the most successful of the *artistes* that night, and it is my theory that she owed her triumph to that fact that a girl in flounces and feathers may reasonably be expected to take her clothes off, while for a pretty nurse to do so is unexpected and therefore notably more exhilarating.

Delay is also an important element of striptease, in that the longer it takes, the more drawn out will be those exquisite agonies suffered by the audience. The general technique employed to this end is for a performer to pretend to remove an article of clothing and then not do so, a trick which may be repeated several times before the final exposure. Less common is the device of wearing several versions of the same garment, one atop the other, so that when the *artiste* removes, say, her chemise, she lays bare not the naked splendour of her bosom but merely another, more abbreviated chemise. The greatest exponent of this technique was undoubtedly Mlle F--- l- D-----, who used to take to the stage at *La Chèvre d'Or* in Paris wearing boots, two hats, three evening gowns, four pairs each of gloves and stockings, five corsets, six pairs of combinations, and seven sets of chemises and drawers; the slow removal of which caused more than one Parisian gentleman to pass beyond rapture to a state in which he required neither a waiter nor a doctor, but a mortician.

An alternative style of striptease is for the performer to pretend that she is removing her clothes accidentally, or better still, has no choice but to do so. The commonest form of this is for a girl to pretend to be disrobing for her bath, her bed or a lover, as if unaware of the presence of a large audience not infrequently including a brass band. Then there is the classic example known as *La Puce*, in which the performer pretends that she is suffering the attentions of a notably belligerent flea, forcing her to remove her clothing one article at a time until she is stark naked. Rather more inventive, I felt, was Mlle F--- l- C---'s performance, *La Petite Voleuse*, which I saw in Tours last year, in which she played the accomplice to a scheming young man who, on the pretext of stealing apples from an orchard, persuades her out of her clothes that they may carry ever more fruit until, when she is naked and endeavouring to pick up her burdens, he is able to surprise her from behind.

Electrostimulation

The use of mild electrical impulses to stimulate the skin for purposes of arousal, and an example of the abuse of invention for carnal purposes.

This is no simple matter, and also serves to illustrate the extraordinary lengths deviants will go to in order to indulge their beastliness. Considerable knowledge of physics is required in order to construct an electrostimulation device, and both exact judgement and no small amount of luck required to ensure that the balance of volts and amps remains within tolerable boundaries.

Despite these difficulties, such devices exist, and indeed, are not especially rare. I have observed twenty-seven, each of unique design, and in fifteen cases been able to make a more or less detailed investigation. A typical example is that machine constructed by Dr E---- v-- H----- of Rotterdam in Holland. It consists of a squat table, on which is mounted an elaborate system of interconnected armatures, cogs, wheels, levers and glass bulbs. I do not pretend to understand the exact purpose of each component, but by the vigorous turning of a large handle, a task undertaken by his assistant, I---, it is possible to accumulate an electrostatic charge at the tip of a rod. A selection of heads are available for this rod, made of glass or metal and cunningly shaped to suit the most sensitive areas of the body, male and female. When brought close to the skin, these heads release their charge in the form of purple sparks, which create a marked tingling sensation and can bring a woman to a state of erotic hysteria within a remarkably short time, certainly shorter than it takes I--- to tire of turning his wheel.

As is common practice among deviants of a scientific bent, Dr E---- v-- H----- claims that his invention is primarily for medical rather than erotic purposes, although as he also seeks to claim that there are medical benefits to erotic hysteria the distinction is perhaps moot. *See fig. 12*

{Fig. 12} 'To illustrate the extraordinary lengths deviants will go to in order to indulge their beastliness'

Epitrolagnia

The desire to inspect, or to be inspected, for carnal purposes.

Miss A----- T---- of Kendal in Lancashire, for example, requires that her lovers make a full inspection of her naked body and deliver a flattering report of considerable length, which they are obliged to read out loud before she allows them to proceed to more conventional depravities. She is said to be a stern critic, and if unimpressed to have gentlemen tied down by her grooms so that she may seat herself on their heads, which she imagines to be a punishment of sorts, but has led to her gaining a reputation with præfocophiliacs from as far afield as Lexington and Rangoon.

This is also commonly associated with military fetishists. The notorious fourth Lord G-----, for example, would regularly parade his female troops in varying states of undress according to the clemency of the weather. He was keen on drill, and took particular pleasure in having the girls dress and undress as fast as possible, with a public flogging reserved for the most tardy, but his principal joy lay in inspecting them. This he did with what many would consider an unnecessary attention to detail, using a large magnifying glass to asses the condition of everything from their hair to their toes, but with particular attention to their bosoms. While doing this he is said to have been in the habit of making copious notes, to such an extent that when his son burnt them after his Lordship's death the resulting pyre was visible several miles away and caused the local militia to turn out in the belief that we were being invaded by the French.

Equitolagnia

Not to be confused with Equus Eroticus, this practice revolves around the riding of horses and more importantly the necessary accoutrements thereunto. While not uncommon, this practice has become idealised to the extent that it is possible to construct the perfect image for both male and female equitolagniacs.

The woman is tall, elegant, with long legs, a slender waist and a bosom of moderately full development. She is beautiful, in a somewhat stern fashion, but her face is hidden beneath a veil depending from a smart top hat. She wears a tailored riding habit, long boots of fine leather, gloves of the same, and carries a silver-tipped riding crop. Her attire is uniformly black, her sole concession to colour being the vivid red of her painted lips.

The gentleman is taller still and possessed of an upright, military bearing. He has considerable dash and rides with flair and bravery verging on recklessness, while his attire is that of the English country huntsman, typically with a pink rather than a black coat. As with his female counterpart, he carries a riding crop.

As evidence of the popularity of these twin images, I cite the frequency with which both occur in sensationalist literature and illustrated magazines, while I have found that in no less than thirty-four in a hundred cases the favourite onanistic fantasy of country maids is to be seduced by a masterful equestrian, while a further six in a hundred prefer to imagine succumbing to the sapphic embraces of his female counterpart.

Equus Eroticus

Generally known as 'pony-play' or 'pony-girls', this is a most elaborate depravity in which the female, or occasionally the male, is treated in the manner of a horse or pony (*Equus caballus*). While at first glance this might seem peculiar in the extreme, this is in fact a corruption of our English love for healthy equestrian sports and as such is commoner than might be expected, especially among the upper echelons of society.

In the male, Equus Eroticus is thought to originate from the normally harmless practice of riding nanny, or perhaps an elder sister, in the nursery, from which the depraved mind may derive sexual association upon arriving at adulthood. Others, of a less instinctive nature, may simply find the practice a convenient means of expressing other depravities, notably exhibitionism, dominance, bondage and flagellation, but also mudlarking and a variety of forms of erotic humiliation.

In the female, by contrast, this form of beastliness generally derives from close association and identification with ponies, of which girls of breeding are notably fond. Thus, having come to admire equine characteristics in all innocence, the lure of the depraved gentleman who wishes to indulge that admiration for his own ends may prove too strong to resist.

Once a relationship has been established, for this is not a solitary vice, the couple find a broad range of opportunities open to them. The simplest of these, and often the starting point on the road of seduction, is for the gentleman to ride upon the lady's back. This may be done clothed, and in more Bohemian circles has on occasion been passed off as a parlour game. It is also a ruse by which both male and female proponents of the depravity may seek their counterparts.

From simple back riding a path leads by degrees to open debauchery. The first step is generally for the female, or pony-girl, to remove her clothing. For the male, or master, the aim will be the display of her charms, while for her being naked allows greater verisimilitude, as horses do not habitually go clothed. Therefore the succession from full modesty, through the display of undergarments to complete exposure may be achieved with unusual rapidity.

Now that the seducer has his victim naked and in the role of a pony-girl he may indulge himself to the full, either in erotic congress with his bare-back mount or in the wide variety of elaborations associated with this penchant. These may be used separately or in combination, as practicality and the desires of the couple dictate.

Harness is frequently employed, but due to the physiological differences between Equids and womankind this must be adapted or, more usually, custom made. A typical pony-girl harness will consist of headstall, bridle, girth and chest straps, and is generally designed to display rather than conceal the bosom and posterior. Boots are also commonly employed, sometimes with the forward part made as a hoof, while a leather or rubber mouth bit serves both for control and as a gag. Saddles exist in two forms. The conventional saddle rests on the pony-girl's back and is attached by a girth strap, allowing her master to ride on her, whereas the racing saddle is a small seat resting on the upper slopes of her posterior and attached to a substantial body harness, a system practical only if the pony-girl is substantially larger than her rider. Blinkers, kicking straps, lunge reins, traces and anything else more normally associated with equestrianism may be employed to choice. For those for whom restraint is an important element of pony-play, the girl may be made to wear mittens or have her arms bound or encased in a long, leather sheath known as a monoglove.

Many enthusiasts of Equus Eroticus enjoying decorating their pony-girls, and harness may be adapted to allow the attachment of brasses, rosettes, bells and head-dresses of ribbon or ostrich feathers, also elaborate hairstyles. Such accessories serve to enhance the experience for both participants, allowing the pony-girl the expression of her natural vanity and her master the corresponding satisfaction.

Most distinctive, and most depraved, among accessories is the pony-girl tail. This consists of a hank of hair, ideally matching that on her head, which is positioned as if it were a horse's tail. Three forms exist. The tail may attach to the rear of the pony-girl's girth strap, so that it appears to protrude from the base of her spine in realistic and elegant fashion. The tail may attach by means of a plug inserted between the pony-girl's posteriors and deeper still, an unutterably depraved and inelegant solution suitable only for the crawling position. A rather more elegant technique is for the tail to attach to a plug and shaft arrangement, so that it appears to emerge from the base of the pony-girl's spine and is secured both within her fundamental aperture and to the rear of her girth strap, or by means of a fine catgut belt, a system invented by a Mr B---- of Messrs J--- and G----- B---- of Ringwood, who are indeed the leading outfitters for all such paraphernalia.

Having harnessed and attired his pony-girl to his satisfaction, the master may then enjoy her in a variety of ways, either alone or in the company of his fellow enthusiasts. Pony-girls are notably popular in the field of erotic sport, and she may be shown, exercised, trained to perform feats of dressage, jumped or raced, but the most popular usage is to harness her to a small cart, which she can then pull with her master riding in comfort.

Such carts are generally sulkies or gigs equipped with paired shafts, although at least one three-seater carriage is known to exist, this with pole gear and swingletrees to permit the harnessing of a two-, four- or even six-in-hand, a contraption which, in defiance of law, order and all good taste, has been driven through the streets of London.

Discipline is generally an important part of pony-play and, as might be expected, this is effected with the appropriate implements, riding crops, carriage and dressage whips and so forth, although spurs are considered unreasonably cruel by all but the most depraved. When riding or driving, the whip may be applied to the pony-girl's back or legs, but as always when it comes to the discipline of women, the posteriors are the favoured target. This may be done for punishment, as an element of training, to urge her to greater efforts during a race or for its own sake.

In rare instances the above may apply in reverse, with the female as mistress and the male as her pony-boy, while both sapphic and lavenderistic pony-play has also been recorded. As is not unusual with such depraved practices, pony-play is not necessarily a mere prelude to erotic congress but a means unto itself; however, in the classic form, once the girl has been stripped, harnessed and ridden or driven, she is then mounted.

Erotic Hysteria

A condition observed only in the female but mimicking the physical responses observed in the male at the point of emission; including the vigorous contraction of certain muscles, hot flushes of the skin, laboured breathing, cries and a tendency to utter profanities. In the male, all of this is evidently necessary as the culmination of the act of congress, while the associated pleasure plays an important part in what drives him to reproduce. Why, however, should there be an equivalent reaction in the female, but only in the female of debauched character?

Many great minds have pondered on the reason for erotic hysteria, considering it from a philosophical, a scientific and, not least, a theological perspective. For example, Dr H---- P---, a physiologist of the modern school, considers it a redundancy, occurring in the female as a counterpoint to emission in the male, much as the male possesses redundant teats in counterpoint to female teats, which are as essential to the continuation of human life as is emission. This is superficially plausible, and there may be an element of truth in it, but it fails to explain why erotic hysteria is not observed among virtuous women.

The same objection confounds the theory of Herr L----- B----, of Wissembourg in Germany, who speculates that the pleasure involved may draw women to desire an act otherwise unthinkable to any person of moral probity, and that it may therefore be seen as a reward, exactly as with the male. This is plainly false, as the virtuous woman need merely submit herself to her husband's embrace, secure in the knowledge that in the eyes of the Lord dutiful matrimony is a state second only in virtue to chastity.

My own theory is simple and explains the observed facts, in accordance with accepted scientific practice. Erotic hysteria is given not by God, for if this was the case it would plainly be reserved for virtuous woman rather than the reverse, but is a device designed to lure the susceptible into vice and depravity, and not a gift at all, but an affliction born of Beelzebub.

Erotoaplistia

May be defined as being open to erotic congress with both the opposite sex and one's own, although within this definition lies considerable scope for variety. Certain authorities, including Dr S------ F---- of Vienna, have speculated that this represents an intermediate stage between ordinary behaviour and lavenderism or sapphism, depending on sex, but my own observations show that those of erotoaplistiac habit tend to remain so, and that therefore it is more properly explained by pure licentious greed, hence the term I choose to apply.

Consider, for instance, Mrs P-----, of Ludlow in Shropshire. Widowed at an early age, she was left in possession of a large fortune and loose morals, both passed on by her late husband, Mr A----- P-----, who was apparently in the habit of setting up lewd *tableaux vivants* between his wife and assorted servants. These tableaux included elements of both sapphic and lavenderist practice, as they had done with the gentleman's two previous wives. On his death, his widow is known to have kept what appears to have been a remarkable carnal appetite satiated with a long series of footmen and maids, her specific preference being for one of each, taken simultaneously. Thus we observe Mr A----- P----- displaying this habit for over forty years and his wife for over fifty, with neither of them showing a marked preference for one sex or the other. As I say, pure licentious greed.

F

Fetters/Shackles/Manacles

Devices consisting of cuffs for wrists, ankles, neck or even waist, connected by chains or bars, made of either iron or brass and designed to impose restriction of movement upon the human body. Ordinary fetters were once in widespread use, notably in that most regrettable of human practices the slave trade, but are now officially restricted to Her Majesty's prisons, and even there not so widely used as they once were. As devices of erotic bondage they still, however, enjoy considerable popularity and may generally be distinguished from the ordinary form by the presence of leather or even fur padding to prevent chafing of the skin. This remains true even when the items in question are designed for men, a typical example of the unmanly attitudes prevalent among the debauched.

This subject also provides illustration of the deplorable tendency of those in commerce to place financial expediency before morality. In Sheffield, the firm of B---------- and S---- were long known as the pre-eminent suppliers of fetters to both the slave trade and prisons both within the British Isles and beyond. On the abolition of the slave trade within our imperial domains one might have expected them to cease production, and perhaps make some appropriate gesture of remorse. Instead they opened a factory in Birmingham, Alabama.

Both factories continue to operate to this day, and in order to offset the gradual decline in demand for their product, they now produce an extensive line of padded cuffs. These have proved so successful that nowadays their commercial travellers are as likely to be found visiting brothels as prisons, and many times during my investigations I have noted the discreet mark of 'B&S, Sheffield' imprinted on a velvet-lined cuff fastened around the wrist or ankle of some lady of negotiable virtue.

Figging

A practice hard to describe without exceeding all bounds of propriety. Suffice to say that the intention is to further exaggerate those feelings naturally attendant upon the application of a cane to a lady's posteriors by use of a small hourglass-shaped plug carved from the rhizome of *Zingiber officinale*, that monocotyledonous perennial generally known as ginger. This object, the 'fig', is placed exactly where you might expect it to be by the sort of despicable rake who would cane a girl for pleasure. This, so I am assured, gives rise to a strong burning sensation, the effects of which are squirming, a curious treading motion of the feet, wriggling of the toes and an inability to properly tighten the posterior muscles.

This is a technique most frequently employed by the sort of rakes and roués who are not content merely to apply erotic chastisement to their subjects but wish to steal away every last trace of modesty. Even the most debauched of young ladies generally dread the insertion of a fig, although more often than not with excited apprehension rather than unalloyed fear. Miss L--- F------, for instance, an unashamed enthusiast for the cane, has been known to play cards with her fellow maids with a figging and six of the best reserved as forfeit. A piece of ginger and a fruit knife are placed on a saucer at the centre of the table, so that all may see what is to be the fate of the unfortunate loser. Attention to the game is keen, and while each girl will try her hardest to win, I have frequently observed more disappointment than relief on the faces of those who manage to evade punishment.

Fimonolagnia

More generally referred to as flagellation, this involves physical chastisement with one or more of a wide range of purposefully designed implements ordinarily used for correction but for the purposes of this work for carnal stimulation. Individual implements are examined separately, but the basic principles must also be considered.

These are threefold: the sense of exposure and resulting shame, the pain associated with being struck, and the resultant heating of the blood, all of which, by that curious reversal of common sense so typical of the beastly, cease to be unpleasant sensations and instead become the source of carnal excitement. Thus do the depraved come to crave what any right-thinking person would abhor.

While the erotic flagellant is no doubt dead to all sense of decency, he, or she, is not necessarily the dull vulgarian one might suppose. Their practices are often elaborate and occasionally elegant. Nor is erotic flagellation simply a case of the strong flogging the weak for their vicious amusement. Indeed, the number of those craving flagellation exceeds those whose pleasure is in wielding the whip by nearly three to one.

Despite the moral values in our great nation being the highest among all mankind, flagellant practice is astonishingly common. I have observed it among every class, and in every region of the British Isles, and would venture to suggest that so decadent has our society become that whenever a posterior is smacked there is more likely to be some element of arousal, albeit hidden, than otherwise.

Take, for example, the female members of the family and staff at B------- H--- in Berkshire. Lady B------- herself maintains discipline by the occasional application of a cane to her housekeeper's posteriors. The housekeeper, in turn, uses a birch upon the senior parlourmaid, who, in her own turn, employs a hairbrush to keep the junior parlourmaid on her toes. The junior parlourmaid uses a carpet beater on the posteriors of the tweenie maid, who in turn spanks both scullery maids, while these last three are also smacked with a wooden spoon by the cook. No doubt you are thinking that such a system of domestic discipline is typical of an English country house and no cause for alarm, but closer inspection of these arrangements has allowed me to ascertain that following these chastisements depraved acts occur between the participants in thirty-seven cases out of the hundred, and have involved everybody from the scullery maids to Lady B------- herself.

Fundoadoria

The practice of treating the female posterior as an object of veneration. This is a remarkably common paraphilia in males, reported in thirty-five per hundred among those of a sufficiently carnal nature to admit to such things. Several variants exist, the simplest of which is for the female to display her exposed posterior to suitable advantage while the watching male stimulates himself, usually prior to further related sexual activity, although in extreme cases the adoration of his accomplice's rear charms may represent the culmination of desire. More commonly, the male will kiss or lick the female, often in the most fervent and unrestrained manner.

Fundoadoria is also recorded in the sapphic form, in which case it is usual for the ladies to take turns in the enjoyment of each other's posteriors. This may also be done in a spirit of perverse mischief to incite male admiration, and is not infrequently a component of sapphic burlesque, such as that which is the speciality of the house of Madame F--- M-----, at 21, Rue de Tours in Orléans, France. In order to excite the admiration of her clients, Madame M----- has her girls parade in the centre of the salon, first fully clothed, then with their skirts lifted, then their petticoats also, and finally with their drawers held wide to display their naked posteriors, each and every one of which is of the finest quality, having been personally selected by Madame

{Fig. 13} 'Having been personally selected by Madame herself'

herself, and also powdered, rouged and creamed. Thus displayed, the girls play with
each other in the most lewd fashion, stroking, smacking, kissing and even licking
each others' beautiful posteriors, until one by one the men lose all restraint and the
girls are taken upstairs for yet more intimate indulgences. *See fig. 13*

Furniture Bondage

A most peculiar subdivision of bondage which involves the subject being tied up,
not so much in order to restrain him or her, but so that they may be utilised as
an item of furniture, most frequently a small table or a footstool.

Sir M----- D----, the notorious lavenderist, for instance, used to tie his young
conquests into a number of positions, invariably using precise techniques
and carefully selected cords of various colours so as to be sure of achieving an
æsthetically pleasing effect. Typically, he would have a footstool, a table for drinks
and another on which to place his paper and spectacles, and a stand for his hat
and coat, all composed of young men he had persuaded to vice, including, in one
instance, the Marquess of T------ on the night before his wedding.

Less well known but even more inventive, is the widow of the late Dr E-----
G-----, who has employed a proportion of her husband's wealth to install electrical
lighting in her Mayfair home. An enthusiast for furniture bondage and also an
agalmatophiliac and sadist, she has installed her young paramour, Mr S-------- S-----,
as a light fitting, with a wooden helmet of curious design to hold the bulb and shade,
a system of polished brass fetters to ensure his immobility, and a cord attached to his
virile member as a switch, cunningly fastened so that only by maintaining himself
in a state of permanent excitement can he keep the light on and avoid incurring the
displeasure of his mistress, which is said to be keen.

G

Gambling

A vice beastly enough in itself but more beastly still when employed as an agent of seduction. I have seen this done many times, generally in houses of ill repute and at the meetings of licentious societies, when the outcome makes little difference save as to who pays whom, how much is paid and the precise nature of whatever beastliness follows. Regrettably, I have also witnessed it among otherwise respectable but inadequately chaperoned parties of young ladies.

The behaviour of the rake in such circumstances follows a predictable pattern. From the start he makes himself as agreeable as he knows, for the art of charm is bread and butter to the successful seducer. He provides strong drink, often Champagne with a dash of brandy, which cocktail I believe to be more efficacious than any other when it comes to making a lady forget herself. Once a merry atmosphere has developed and he judges the ladies to be adequately inebriated, he proposes a game of cards, bridge, whist, cribbage or whatever it might be, but insists on small stakes to make the game interesting.

Skill at cards is as much a part of the rake's armoury as liquor and charm, and he will be able to balance the game so that it remains interesting while ensuring that the prettiest of the girls, or those he judges to be most pliable, swiftly loose their all. At this point, amidst much laughter and badinage, he will state that he is prepared to accept a kiss in place of his winnings. Seldom is such a request rejected, for it seems harmless enough, but this is only the first small step along the path to depravity.

As he continues to play, this odious fellow will introduce yet more intimate forfeits, first the removal of small articles such as gloves or shoes, then major apparel, which he frequently uses as an excuse to lure his prey from the gaming table and upstairs to her fate. However, I have seen such games continue further still, the girls paying forfeit with their most intimate garments, and in one case leaving no less than five of the prettiest young things imaginable sat still around a table in no more than corsets and stockings, with one stark naked, all to the immense satisfaction of the gloating rake.

In sharp contrast was the occasion on which Miss J------- M-------- had just been teased into opening her chemise when her father and brothers entered the room, back from a shooting party, and the rake in question was forced to flee incontinent, dodging buckshot as he crossed the lawns and not altogether successfully. It is a dangerous game the seducer plays, and many have come to a sorry end, none more so perhaps than a certain licentious young curate who shall remain nameless.

He had followed the pattern as laid out above, while in company of a number of young ladies in the American city of New York, but while their virtue proved easy enough to overcome, the same was not true of their skill at cards. Thus, instead of enjoying the gradual process of getting them stripped down, he soon found himself stark naked, upon which the most boisterous of his companions suggested spankings as forfeits. In the circumstances he could hardly refuse, especially as there seemed every opportunity of enjoying the spectacle of a playful sapphic encounter as one young lady was placed across another's knee, but it was not to be. He continued to lose, and before long found himself in one corner, stark naked and tied into an awkward position across a chair, gagged, blindfolded and with his posteriors copiously reddened, while behind him, invisible but entirely audible, the girls disported themselves in an orgy of giggling sapphic depravity, a keen fate but admittedly not without justice.

Gerontophilia

A false paraphilia meaning the obsessive desire for those markedly older than oneself, which is evidently a nonsense.

A paraphilia may be defined by the fact of its being irrational and ungodly, in that the carnal energies become diverted from procreation towards some other point of focus. For what has been termed gerontophilia, this is manifestly not the case. What could be wiser than for a young girl to choose as her mate not some naive young swain with neither maturity, nor judgement, nor a sufficiency of worldly goods, but a man of mature years and seasoned judgement, with stability of character and the accumulated wealth of a lifetime?

Glaciolagnia

The use of ice for carnal stimulation, notably upon the female bosom and frequently in conjunction with hot wax, creating an effect beloved of sensualists.

The primary requirement of this fetish is ice, and it is therefore seasonal, save in the very coldest of latitudes and among those of sufficient wealth to maintain an ice house or to purchase that peculiar device known as the 'refrigerator', a term coined by the engineer Mr T----- M---- in 1800. Mr M---- was not, however, a glaciolagniac, to the best of my knowledge, nor was he the first to produce ice by scientific methods. That honour, although the word is perhaps inappropriate in this case, must go to Dr T------- S----, in 1761, who was a glaciolagniac, and appears to have spent over thirty years and a considerable part of his fortune in an effort to build a machine that would allow him to ice his wife's teats out of the normal season. If contemporary records are to be believed, Dr S----'s machine was the height of a two-storey townhouse, weighed some eighteen tons, required four men to operate it and when in operation could be heard five miles away from the village of Cropwell Bishop, where he lived. Such are the extremes to which the debauched are prepared to go in order that they may indulge their beastliness, although it should also be noted that Dr S---- was quite mad.

Gommory

That sin for which God destroyed the city of Gommorah. It is not entirely clear what this involved, but it was certainly beastly.

Gounaphilia

The need, or desire, for fur in order to achieve carnal arousal. This is a common paraphilia with two principal subdivisions: females who enjoy intimate contact with fur, and males who enjoy their lovers wearing fur.

These last are frequently of a submissive or masochistic nature, and indeed Herr L------ v-- S------M----- himself was a confirmed gounaphiliac, although why the dominant female should be associated with fur is not immediately clear, lest it be that she thus seems to take on the savage, primordial characteristics of the early hunter, or perhaps those of the slain beast who originally wore the fur. This last theory would be more tenable if the commonest fur in use both commercially and among gounaphiliacs was not that of the common European rabbit (*Oryctolagus cuniculus*).

The female gounaphiliac does not, generally, pursue other paraphilias, but is focused purely on her love of fur for its own sake. She will wear fur, sleep on fur, upholster her furniture with fur, and, most significantly, indulge her private passions on fur. Thus, for example, we have Miss C------ D------, who does all these things, including having her drawers, corset and chemise not merely trimmed with fur, but lined. She also possesses fur stockings, fur-trimmed petticoats, several fur dresses and innumerabal fur coats, stools and wraps made from such an extensive array of animals that her principal paramour, a noted big game hunter, is obliged to spend much of his time abroad in the search for more. Her bed is also spread with furs and yet others cover the floors of her Belgravia mansion. Furthermore, when she invites a lover to her house, he is obliged to indulge her fantasy by dressing up in fur, so that he comes to the conjugal bed looking as if he were an exceptionally well groomed caveman.

A subdivision of this, known as *Pilosus Eroticus*, relates to animal transformation fantasy, whereby the subject is not content merely with wearing fur or having another wear fur, but goes to the extreme of donning a fur suit in imitation of the original animal, most frequently a big cat such as the jaguar (*Felis onca*) or leopard (*Felis pardus*), but I have also recorded human wolves, bears, beavers and, in one case, the Australian marsupial wombat, only not the common wombat (*Phascolomys platyrhinus*), but the Hairy-Nosed Wombat (*Phascolomys latifrons*).

Governess

A post not normally associated with depravity, rather the opposite, but certain important exceptions exist and must be duly noted.

So strong is the bond between governess and charge that on occasion it can give way to obsession, and if this should last into adult life complications may arise. I have recorded more than a dozen instances of this, including two lavenderistic and one sapphic example, but the clearest illustration is without doubt the regrettable case of Sir C---- T-------, a man whose life has been a model of probity and restraint in every aspect save one. On his Warwickshire estate he employs a number of staff, including a governess, Miss W-----, and yet the youngest of his children has long ago attained adulthood and is, I believe, currently engaged in fighting the Boers in southern Africa. Miss W----- is a tall, stately lady, exceptionally slender and angular in her features, creating an impression of stern rectitude which is reflected in her personality. She wears nothing but black.

It was while visiting my bootmakers, Messrs H----- & C------, in Northampton that this first came to my attention, when I happened to glance at their work book and noticed an order from Sir C---- for thigh-length boots of soft black leather to be fitted with steel heel pieces five inches in height. These were to be considerably too small for Sir C---- himself, but I nevertheless suspected depravity, and upon investigation this proved to be the case.

There is, it turns out, a locked room on the third floor of Sir C----'s mansion, although a dense growth of ivy on the south wall allows a person of righteous determination to gain access to a window. In this room, the Baronet takes daily lessons, in mathematics, geometry, Latin and presumably other subjects, all under the tutelage of Miss W----, who loses no opportunity in wielding the cane or tawse for even the most trifling of errors, and also seems notably short of temper, frequently dishing out vigorous spankings for no apparent reason. I will grant that Sir C----'s scholastic performance is poor, and he no doubt benefits from this tuition, but I cannot approve the manner in which it is given, nor Miss W----'s practice of concluding the lesson with a firm spanking followed by an act of manual stimulation with the Baronet still held firmly across her knees.

Gravidophilia

In men a marked preference for women heavy with child, and the heavier the better. In women, a tendency to experience erotic hysteria when heavy with child.

In either case this is distinctly improprietous, for gravidity should be treated with appropriate gravity, and not made the object of depraved lusts, however frequently it may be the result thereof. The thought of a woman caressing her swollen belly as she indulges herself in a long and slow session of onanism is particularly disturbing. However, I cannot entirely condemn this practice, for unlike the great majority of beastly behaviour it is conducive to holy matrimony, for how else may a male gravidophiliac come to regularly enjoy his obsession than by taking a wife?

Some, however, can go too far. Mr S----- Q------, for example, was, as a young man, considered a model of both industry and propriety. He studied hard and worked hard, rising from obscurity to become the largest eel smoker in his native Boston and taking as his wife Miss A--- B----, the daughter of a local crab fisherman. Before another ten years had passed Q------'s nutritious eel and crab paste was to be found in every emporium of quality in the country and the Empire beyond, to say nothing of several European countries, including the Scandanavian, most of which he insisted on visiting personally and at frequent intervals. Only on his death were the true facts discovered, that he had not one wife, but nine, in locations as far apart as Bilbao and Bombay, and that these had, in the course of the years, borne him no fewer than seventy-six children, at an average of approximately eight and four tenths per wife.

This struck me as peculiar at the time, and so I requested access to his business records. After some considerable effort I managed to deduce that he had timed his expeditions so that as often as possible he would be with any given wife in the seventh or eighth month of her time, thus revealing him as not only a nonagamist but an obsessive gravidophiliac.

Grope Box

A device of truly devilish depravity, designed to allow the subject to be fondled without restraint and frequently unaware of whose hands are in contact with his, or her, flesh.

In construction, the grope box is simple: a large cube, with one face hinged to form a door, big enough for one person to fit inside with moderate comfort, perhaps even fitted with a seat, but too small to allow escape from the reach of arms poked

{Fig. 14} 'This is said to greatly stimulate Madame M------'s trade'

into the numerous holes cut in each side. As might be expected, such devices are most frequently found in use by those societies dedicated to carnal debauchery, among whom it is common practice to place a girl in such a box, either naked or in her underwear so that a game may be made of removing what remains of her clothes.

I have also noted a variation on this theme in use at the establishment of Madame F--- l- M------, at 32, Rue Marshal Ney in Nancy, where a squat box sits to one side of the salon. This is crafted to resemble a die, with the appropriate holes cut in the sides. A girl is placed in the box, kneeling in such a fashion that her head protrudes from that hole corresponding to the one, while visitors to the brothel roll dice for the privilege of inserting their hands through the two, three, four and five holes that surround her so that they may fondle her for a space before the game continues. This is said to greatly stimulate Madame M------'s trade. *See fig. 14*

H

Handcuffs

Locking metal fetters employed by Her Majesty's Constabulary in the apprehension of malefactors and by the depraved for purposes of restraint. Indeed, handcuffs are seldom employed as a simple accessory, and more often as part of an elaborate erotic diversion, whereby the gentleman participant pretends to be a policeman and affects a mock arrest upon the lady, first placing her in handcuffs and then disporting himself upon her body in whatever manner he desires.

Mr E----- H----, of Steeple Felching in the county of Rutland, extends this practice somewhat further. Dressed as an Inspector of police, with his butler as the sergeant and his three footmen as constables, along with the occasional guest, he pursues his maids through the woods of his estate. When caught, the hapless girls are put in handcuffs, with their arms around the bole of a suitable tree, thus rendering them powerless to resist his caresses and the injection of his virile member, all of which is done while the servants look on. *See fig. 15*

Harapaxophilia

An extremely rare paraphilia in which the subject achieves carnal arousal by virtue of being robbed, or committing a theft.

It might be argued that the latter form of this is commonplace among men who seek trophies of their conquests or collect items of ladies' apparel. However, in the majority of such instances that I have recorded, the pleasure either comes from making the collection or lies in the undergarments themselves, and the fact that they are stolen is secondary. Some, however, are borderline cases, and I recall Sir

{Fig. 15} 'Mr E----- H----, of Steeple Felching in the county of Rutland, extends this practice somewhat further'

H---- H--------, who, after showing me his extensive collections of ladies' corsets, each stolen from a paramour as she slept, grew sufficiently warm that he was obliged to relieve himself upon the chambermaid, greatly to my embarrassment.

True harapaxophilia appears to be largely a female paraphilia, although with so few cases documented it is impossible to draw firm conclusions. Mrs V--- P-----, however, provides an excellent illustration of this practice. Determined to assuage a desire which had been growing within her for many years, she waited until her husband was abroad on military service and then arranged, with the assistance of her lady's maid, for the house to be burgled one night. She was most specific in her requirements, stating that the burglar should be above six feet in height, of powerful build and comely appearance, below thirty years of age and of exceptional virile development. The event was also intended as a surprise, a crucial element of her desire, and thus when she awoke to the noises from the lower part of the house in the early hours of one morning she went down to investigate with no more trepidation than is normal in a young woman about to fulfil a depraved penchant. As expected, the burglar was there, and after a moment of surprise took advantage of her apparent shock and state of partial disrobal by taking her vigorously from behind across the grand piano. Only later did she discover that her maid had been unable to find a subject of the required specifications, and that the man to whom she had surrendered was a real burglar, although it should be noted that her complaints commenced only after this discovery.

Harness

Any system of cloth, leather or occasionally metal straps used to control beasts of burden, or in the case of the depraved, their fellow human beings. Carnal harness is generally used as an adjunct to pony-play and other animal transformation fantasies, which are treated separately, but exceptions exist.

Suspension harness is one such, and allows the subject to be suspended in the air, usually a woman, and usually at a height convenient for the insertion of the virile member of the male participant. Other examples allow the subject to be suspended upside down or in a variety of convoluted positions, as often as not from motives of pure sadism.

Perhaps the most peculiar example of harness I have ever come across was that employed by Mr V----- P---- of Exeter for the furtherance of his highly peculiar penchant. He was obsessed with metamorphosis, and wished to be enclosed in the manner of a cocoon or chrysalis and suspended from the rafters in the attic of his town house. To this end he designed and constructed an elaborate harness that would support his silk-wrapped body in comfort for several hours, along with a cunning latch so that at the supreme moment he could emerge, complete an act of erotic congress with Miss S--- W--------, a lady of negotiable virtue he had employed specifically for this purpose, and then feign a dramatic death in order to complete what he anticipated as the supreme experience of his life. This was not to be, as the latch jammed, and Miss W--------, having grown bored with the procedure, had left to take a cup of tea with a friend who lived nearby. It was two days before Mr P---- was discovered, by which time he had been comprehensively cured of his obsession.

Hogtie

A distinctive form of bondage popular in those rural areas noted for pig farming, and especially Wiltshire.

The essence of the hogtie is for the wrists and ankles to be bound together in the manner of a pig made ready for market, although in the case of a man or woman this means that the legs are flexed upwards and the arms stretched down behind the back, joining at the posteriors. This is an uncomfortable position, and appears to be of little practical value from the erotic perspective, save for those who consider restraint to be of value for its own sake. By logical extension it should also be possible to truss somebody in those manners typically used for chicken, duck or perhaps rabbit and hare, but I have yet to come across examples of such techniques.

More advanced forms of hogtying include joining the upper arms or thighs with additional rope, fixing the wrists to the waist or thighs, and running a cord between the legs to a waist rope. The subject is generally female, and naked or in no more than a corset; at least, this was the case at a demonstration I recently managed to attend on the pretext of myself being a ligolagniac, where a Mr S--- W-----, of Chalk Brow Farm near Mere, displayed a number of techniques with the kind assistance of his wife and two nieces.

Hoods

Bag-like structures of cloth or leather designed to fit over the head. These are employed for a variety of reasons, but in the case of carnal depravity the intent is to temporarily deprive the subject of their sight, normally in conjunction with bondage, thus allowing him or her to be interfered with at leisure while unaware of who is doing what.

A secondary effect of hooding is to render the subject's face concealed, and thus ensure their anonymity, which is presumably why the practice is notably popular among ladies of quality who wish to indulge their vices without being recognised. Indeed, to my certain knowledge, twice each month the Princess V------- of S--------H------- has herself hooded and taken by closed carriage to a house of ill repute in Hannover, where she is stripped naked save for her hood, tied up and given to any man who cares to pay, at the normal price, thus indulging her penchants for serial depravity and erotic humiliation while remaining safely anonymous, save to those who choose to peer beneath her hood.

Iatrikophilia

The carnal delight in all things medical, a paraphilia of such astonishing variation that no general statement can do it justice, save to say that it is more commonly found in the female than in the male. I therefore present a number of case studies, from the perusal of which the general depravity of the practice may all too easily be appreciated.

Sir C----- V--- of St Anselm's Hospital, Greenwich, has produced an extensive treatise on aberrant desires, which, although taken from clinical observations rather than actual fieldwork, is highly illuminating as regards iatrikophilia. During my period as chaplain to the hospital I was privileged to observe several of his cases, and to read the records of still more. Thus I am able to say with confidence that the commonest form of iatrikophila relates to epitrolagnia, known as inspection fantasy. Typically, a lady will feign a complaint of a private nature so that her intimate parts may be inspected at close quarters by a doctor, thus allowing her the indulgence of her penchant without risk of being accused of impropriety. With some ladies it is the bosom she wishes attended to, with others the legs or the posteriors, but in the great majority of cases it is that most intimate part of all. Miss T------ A--------, for example, maintained a regular monthly appointment for a period of some five years, demanding on every occasion the intimate use of a speculum, and while invariably blushing with embarrassment never once made an objection to the presence of nurses, other doctors, students and, indeed, myself.

Miss A-------- also appears to have enjoyed another facet of this paraphilia in that she quite evidently took pleasure in being a patient, and was invariably in a state of excitement and mild arousal during her visits to the hospital, even when she was not due for her monthly examination. I have observed her, and others, inhale deeply of the scent of disinfectant, touch the material of doctors' coats with what can only be described as a caress, and on one occasion achieve a condition approximating to erotic hysteria while sniffing at a swab soaked in ether.

Notably more beastly are those who crave the helplessness of being confined to bed and the consequent attentions of nurses and other medical staff. A certain rake, Mr B------ W------, used to have himself admitted with complaints carefully judged to ensure a stay of a single night, and in a private room. There, he would select the prettiest of his nurses and appeal to her with a most piteous speech, in which he would claim to be dying and ask for some carnal favour as if it were a final wish. Such is the quality of mercy and sympathy to be found in British nurses that he was almost invariably successful, and on various occasions received manual stimulation beneath the covers, irrumation and even full erotic congress, before he eventually overplayed his hand. On begging a beautiful but rather more experienced sister for an act of proctism, he got precisely what he deserved, a hot oil enema administered with a group of students in attendance.

Some iatrikophiles are also klismolagniacs, and would have actively enjoyed the treatment meted out to Mr W------, while others would have appreciated it for the sake of their own erotic humiliation. Mrs C------- R------- belongs in this latter category, her particular penchant being for injections, which she insisted on taking not in her arm but in one cheek or the other of her posteriors. In this she was quite adamant, and yet she would be blushing fiercely as she raised her skirts and petticoats, unfastened her drawers and exposed herself across Sir V---'s desk to have the needle thrust home and a swab applied to the blemish. I forget what her ailment was, but she attended his surgery at four thirty p.m. each Tuesday for the entire period I was at the hospital.

Iconolagnia

T he enjoyment of pictures or photographs of an erotic nature, an ancient vice made ever more popular by the corruption of inventions.

If proof were needed of the inherently sinful nature of mankind it must lie in the existence of lewd drawings made on the walls of certain caves, and it will not surprise the reader to learn that the majority of such caves are in France. Even the most distant ancestors of the French, it would seem, had an unusual affinity for lewd practices, for let there be no doubt that this is what these pictures depict, despite the claims of certain authorities that they are religious or educational in nature. No, for when a man chooses to depict a woman of improbably ample mammary development on all fours so as to present herself to what I can only hope is a hunter in a wolf skin there can be but one explanation: depravity.

Thus we discover iconolagnia among our most distant forebears, or, at least, among the most distant forebears of the French, and it has continued ever since, with every civilisation known producing lewd depictions to a greater or lesser extent. Only with the coming of Christianity to Europe does this depraved habit reduce, and then only temporarily, for scarcely had the printing press been invented than certain Italians were using it to produce images of erotic congress, a practice which has grown ever since, reaching its peak in the licentious and insurrectionary pamphlets of the French Revolution.

Nor have iconolagniacs, or pornographers as they are commonly known, contented themselves with the corruption of one great invention. No sooner had the photographic process advanced sufficiently to make live studies feasible than some Frenchman persuaded a lady of easy or negotiable virtue out of her clothes so that he might make a series of lewd images. Since then, the proliferation of pornography has known no bounds, with vast quantities of such pictures being produced, showing not merely nudity but every vice imaginable, and sold by shifty fellows of low moral character, most frequently in Paris. I myself, in the course of my researches, have collected no fewer than twelve thousand, four hundred and three unique images, showing everything from ladies in a state of partial undress to the most outrageous depravities known to man.

Ilikialagnia

A form of beastliness in which the submissive participant pretends to be of a different age, generally much younger, thus providing an excuse for the dominant to exert authority, control and often punishment. This is a popular pastime among the debauched, and varies from the merely peculiar to the monstrous.

Costume and setting form an important part of this, and it is not an easy depravity to conceal, with rooms and even entire houses sometimes given over to its indulgence. Therefore it is perhaps not surprising that the practice is largely associated with the wealthier elements of society and that specialised clubs and houses of ill repute exist for ilikialagniacs.

A great many variations of ilikialagnia are recorded, but one predominates, in which male participants take on the role of pupils, as if still at school, but with women of negotiable virtue acting the part of stern mistresses in place of masters. In England alone there are no fewer than five such institutions, at least that I am aware of, all run by enterprising if immoral matrons, three of whom are of genuinely sadistic temperament.

Rather less common is the situation in which a woman adopts the role of a wilful schoolgirl with the man as a master. Thus he may exert his authority over her as he pleases, chastising her and subjecting her to often elaborate humiliations. In a typical situation, the girl might find herself sitting alone at her desk in a room converted to resemble a school classroom. She has been accused of some misdemeanour and awarded a thrashing, a fate on which she is left to dwell while her partner prepares himself. He then enters the room and, after a lecture on her delinquency, a heavy book is placed on her head, which she is obliged to keep steady without the use of her hands. Thus rendered both helpless and awkward, she has her plain woollen school dress lifted and pinned up behind her back, her drawers are opened to expose her posteriors, she is fondled and then thrashed with a cane. Should she drop the book, cry out in her anguish or fail to count the strokes delivered to her unfortunate rear end her punishment is augmented. When it is at last over she is sent into the corner with the book still on her head and her behind naked, until her tormentor is ready to relieve his excitement over her well-whipped posteriors. In the above situation one might reasonably expect the male to be the instigator of such depravity, but my researches show that the reverse is more frequently the case. Indeed, I am able to list three cases, those of Lady A------ C------, Miss L---- N------ and Miss E---- F-------, in which the female participant employs a servant or tradesman to perform the male role, these being, respectively, the butler, her father's chauffeur and a man whose ostensible reason for visiting the house is the sale of religious tracts.

Incarcerophilia

A need to be thrown into prison, something one might well think entirely appropriate for depraved persons were it not for what they wish to happen to them while locked up. Thus, far from wishing to sit in quiet reflection on their sins or to be safely removed from the remainder of the human race, their need is to have their freedom taken away and to be put in the care of harsh and sadistic gaolers.

This is impractical in any real sense, as those few lavenderists who have been foolish enough to make the attempt have speedily discovered. A few houses of ill repute specialise in this service, notably that of Frau M----- G------- in Vienna, who

{Fig. 16} 'Instead chose to live in Paris and invest in cinematography'

has not only cages and a well-equipped dungeon but a row of three cells fitted out in exact imitation of those in the local gaol, or so I am assured. However, in order to fully indulge his, or more rarely her, penchant, an incarcerophiliac needs to be sufficiently wealthy to construct suitable premises and employ suitable staff, while even they must suffer from the knowledge that they could, if necessary, order their own release.

One curious example is worthy of note. Miss L--- W----, a young heiress of Eastbourne in Sussex who might very well have employed her not inconsiderable fortune to enjoy a life of pleasure and make a suitable marriage, instead chose to live in Paris and invest in cinematography. This has, I believe, been at least moderately successful, but her aim is not to enlarge her fortune. She herself takes the central role in her creations, and invariably acts the same part, that of a woman imprisoned and abused by her warders. Thus she is able not only to indulge her penchant for incarceration, but also her klismolagnia, flagellant masochism, ostendophilia, epitrolagnia and xenophilia. *See fig. 16*

Inserviophilia

Commonly referred to as 'erotic slavery', this describes the desire to be the property of another, or, in reverse, to own another, as related to carnal practice. Curiously, and demonstrating an extraordinary lack of shame for their activities, many more claim to practise this paraphilia than actually do. Typically, a person of submissive or masochistic nature, male or female, will exhibit increasing symptoms of inserviophilia as their needs arise, often claiming that their sole purpose in creation is to serve whoever is providing them with stimulation; but, once emission has been achieved, the male at least quickly loses his desire to serve, generally preferring a glass of iced claret or a cup of tea, and not infrequently expecting the woman in question to fetch it, despite having claimed to be her devoted and helpless slave just moments before. Female inserviophiliacs tend to be less contrary in nature, but only marginally so.

The true inserviophiliac wishes their slavery to be absolute, and is characterised by complete dedication to their master or mistress, and complete obedience, including the performance of any erotic act, with any partner and without protest or complaint, simply at the whim of whomsoever they serve. This is rare, but not unknown, and yet I find that even such acts of debasement are ultimately performed primarily for the satisfaction of the inserviophiliac, or in order to provide an excuse for the expression of desires otherwise too base to be contemplated.

I have on several occasions come across a positively blasphemous form of inserviophilia, as exhibited by Mr R------ S------ of Canterbury, who claims that his condition is not a depravity at all, but the highest form of love. This is arrant nonsense, as love, whether deep or shallow, exists as a desire for holy union, a merging of souls, and not the submission of one's will to that of another, nor the reverse. He and his like are depraved, pure and simple, and should be flogged for their vile habits were it not for the fact that they would undoubtedly take pleasure in their chastisement.

Irrumation

The insertion of the virile member into the mouth so that it may be played upon with the lips and tongue. This is an act so monstrously indecent that to any but the utterly depraved it is hard to accept as reality, and yet one I have found to be remarkably common, and not merely among lavenderists, who have by definition already travelled some way down the path to the debauched state, but between men and women.

The process is far from straightforward, and indeed, so many subtle variations exist that no two such acts are ever quite the same, while it is the considered opinion among exponents that a girl requires some years of regular practice before she can fully master the techniques involved. Such details need not concern us here, but suffice to say that for the typical rake or expert lothario, such skills can more than make up for any other shortcomings in their paramours, and some even go so far as to claim that the culminating moment of pleasure can exceed all others.

Nor is this a modern vice. The Romans regarded it with particular horror, using the term *stuprum oris*, among others, but Phœnician women appear to have been guilty of the very grossest of moral turpitude, not merely encouraging the act, but reddening their lips beforehand, the better to mimic that part into which the virile member is more usually inserted.

Japanese Rope Bondage

A rguably the most highly evolved sub-category of bondage, by which the men of that distant and exotic oriental land tie their womenfolk into fantastic contortions using systems of knots and interconnecting ropes which defy the eye to make sense of them. Indeed, some consider the practice to have risen above the level of mere debauchery to that of an art. Nevertheless, the women involved are not infrequently naked or in a state of partial undress, the positions into which they are bound are more generally lewd than not, and, once helpless, the subjects are more often employed for erotic purposes than otherwise. Æsthetically pleasing it may be, but it is still a form of depravity, and having seen some of the extraordinarily elaborate systems of bondage of which our own British tars are capable, I am not convinced of its pre-eminence either.

Indeed, while I witnessed several skilled demonstrations during my time in the Japanese archipelago, on the single occasion on which I have observed it attempted here it was far from successful. A Mr I----- I-------, a Japanese student of some wealth, had arrived at the house of Mrs A--- B----- in Shepherds Market, hired a girl in the normal fashion and paid that premium normally reserved for ligolagniacs. However, so absolute was the tangle in which he rapidly found himself that the young lady in question, a Miss J---- P-----, mistook his intent. After a moment to get over her natural alarm at his struggles and foreign expostulations, which she was quite unable to understand, she concluded that he wished to be bound and punished. She therefore pulled the ropes tight, placed him across her knee with his posteriors exposed and gave him a firm spanking while remonstrating with him for his bad language. *See fig. 17*

{Fig. 17} 'Her natural alarm at his struggles and foreign expostulations'

Jezebelism

The practice of deriving carnal satisfaction specifically from adultery, in one form or another. It may come as no great surprise to learn that this occurs, and that both men and women not only break those vows made together in the presence of the Lord our God but take an active pleasure in both the carnal act itself and the knowledge of their sin. More extraordinary, however, is the related practice of taking pleasure in the erotic congress of one's lawfully wedded wife, or husband, and a third party.

I do not refer here to the mere cuckold, who is more to be pitied than censured, but to those individuals who actively encourage and even watch as their wife or husband indulges in lewd acts, up to and including erotic congress, with a friend, stranger or even a servant. The commonest form of this is for the male to be the observer and, having come to agreement with his wife or lover, to conceal himself in some suitable cupboard or behind a screen, where he will indulge himself in onanistic behaviour while watching his wife and whoever she has selected engaged together in erotic congress or some other depravity.

More rarely, perhaps largely due to the difficulty of arranging matters, the act will be carried out openly, sometimes with the third party making a deliberate display of his actions or even mocking the cuckolded man as he enjoys the lady. One such occasion, I recall, involved Sir J----- M------, an elderly gentleman whose particular pleasure was to watch while his wife entertained a series of sailors from the local naval dockyard, one after the other, although it must be pointed out that he charged a shilling a time and provided only an indifferent claret as refreshment, so it may be that his intentions were financial as well as onanistic, or that the financial element of the transaction further stimulated his peculiar obsession.

K

Kapnophilia

The carnal appreciation of smoking, and of smoking prerequisites. I have recorded three distinct forms of this highly peculiar but relatively mild paraphilia, the commonest of which relates simply to excitement occasioned by those of depraved mind who cannot observe a woman placing any long, thin object in her mouth without immediately wishing it were their virile member instead. Such men tend to have a particularly strong appreciation for painted lips, as do the second group, who take the matter rather further.

These are theaphiles, at least of a sort, who for some unfathomable reason regard a woman with a cigarette in her mouth as an object of adoration. Mr J--- S----- of Dunstable in Bedfordshire provides an excellent example of this, as his idea of carnal enjoyment is to curl up at his wife's feet while she, in immaculate evening dress, smokes a series of cigarettes in an ivory holder of exaggerated length. This has always struck me as a somewhat selfish pleasure, although in this case Mr S----- is also an expert and dedicated kolpolagniac, which must do much to make up for his peculiar requirements.

The third, and most beastly, form of kapnophilia involves the insertion of a cigar into an improper aperture so that it may be smoked in much the same manner as if it were in the mouth, a procedure that argues remarkable muscular control on the part of the woman involved. This is said to be a relatively common practice in the Americas, and the island of Cuba in particular. I have not observed this phenomenon, but once saw a notably stout Sussex farmer perform a not dissimilar operation after spanking his wife, but with the stem of his briar pipe inserted into a yet more unsuitable aperture.

Lastly, there is the related practice, also characteristic of Cuba, whereby some invest with a degree of beastliness the way young girls make cigars by rolling them on the insides of their thighs. Señor S------ D--- of Havana, for example, claims that the taste of individual cigars varies according to who has made them, and that his personal preference is for those rolled on the thigh of a buxom virgin in late afternoon, once she has had time to work up a little perspiration.

Katagelagnia

The practice of deriving erotic pleasure from humiliation, an extraordinarily common phenomenon among the depraved and a concept that goes far to explain what is unimaginable to the virtuous – the desire to debase oneself. How, I am often asked, can anybody, for any inducement whatsoever, willingly perform such shameful acts as I have recorded in this volume? The answer is that much of the pleasure derives from the shame itself, and that therefore the greater the shame, the greater the pleasure.

This is not an assertion I make lightly, but how else are we to explain the behaviour Mr L----- S-----, who returns from his important job in Whitehall to don a suit designed to make him resemble the caterpillar of the Emperor Moth (*Pavonia pavonia*) and thus attired will writhe in onanistic joy on his living-room floor while his wife belabours him with a dog whip? (I feel obliged to point out that he has the anatomy quite wrong, placing two pairs of legs in an anterior position and a further two towards the posterior, rather than the correct combination of three pairs of legs and four pairs of pseudopods.)

Equally puzzling is the case of Miss O---- S----, who designed a summer dress with seams that would tear at the slightest pressure and used to walk regularly on the Surrey Heaths, with the inevitable result that she would be forced to run home in nothing but her combinations and corset, or, on days when exceptional warmth rendered underwear less than strictly necessary, nothing at all.

Yet I do not ask you to accept mere anecdote as proof. Consider, rather, the following experiment, conducted under exact conditions. I have made it a practice

{Fig. 18} 'I feel obliged to point out that he has the anatomy quite wrong, placing two pairs of legs in an anterior position and a further two pairs towards the posterior, rather than the correct combination of three pairs of legs and four pairs of pseudopods'

across the years, when I encounter a maid whom I suspect of depraved tastes, to obtain the permission of her employers to chastise her by means of a vigorous spanking, this involving the full exposure of her posteriors in the presence of an audience and the application of precisely one hundred firm smacks. I have done this many times, and in every single instance the maid, when questioned, has admitted that the procedure was highly shameful. In all cases I have followed the treatment by sending her to her room, there to repent her sins and reflect upon her woes, and on twenty-eight occasions I have been able to observe her subsequent behaviour. In no fewer than thirteen cases out of the twenty-eight instances the smacked maid neither repented her sins nor reflected upon her woes, but instead brought herself to a condition of erotic hysteria. It is true that maids do this in the privacy of their rooms quite often in any case, but in the interests of scientific exactitude I performed a control, sending a number of maids to their rooms without a spanking, and in thirty-one instances only five performed onanistic acts within the first hour of incarceration, which proves my theory beyond reasonable doubt. *See fig. 18*

Katoptronolagnia

The use of mirrors to enhance carnal pleasure. Technically, a true katoptronophiliac should be unable to achieve carnal satisfaction without the use of mirrors, but I have yet to encounter an individual to whom this strictly applies, hence my choice of term. The use of mirrors to support an erotic act by creating a reflection thereof for the enjoyment of those involved is remarkably common, whether that act be onanism, straightforward erotic congress or some other paraphilia.

Narcissistic young men are particularly prone to this vice. Thus we have the example of Mr C---- M-------, an exceptionally comely youth whom I chanced to

{Fig. 19} 'Incapable of performing his conjugal duties without first watching
his young bride undress on the far side of the mirror'

observe while attempting to assess whether or not his sister was guilty of onanistic self-tetigilagnia, which I had long suspected. My initial impression was that he was merely intent on going out for the evening and was a careful dresser, but after he had changed his waistcoat and cravat for the fifth time and had begun to show signs of inappropriate excitement I realised that he was a narcissist. So it proved, as after not less than an hour of self-contemplation in a convenient mirror he proceeded to commit an act of onanistic self-indulgence with one hand while brushing his hair with the other.

We must also include in this category those who use mirrors for nefarious purposes, and in particular as an aid to voyeurism. Dr S--------- C-----, for instance, an eminent physicist of otherwise unimpeachable character, is known to have invented a curious form of mirror whereby one side was reflective but the other transparent. This he installed in the guest bedroom of his villa outside Milan, so that he might invite actresses and singers, for whom he had a particular fondness, and sit at leisure behind his singular invention while he watched them disrobe and perform yet more intimate operations. A salutary lesson may be learned here, for after some years of taking his onanistic satisfaction by this technique the doctor married, only to find himself incapable of performing his conjugal duties without first watching his young bride undress on the far side of his mirror. *See fig. 19*

Kerilagnia

The use of wax for carnal indulgence, and specifically, of molten wax. This is done, or so I understand, by a burning candle being held above the bare skin, sufficiently distant to ensure that there is no risk of burning, but close enough to leave the wax hot as it makes contact, thus causing exactly the sort of mild pain the depraved find so enjoyable.

A perhaps typical kerilagniac was the late Countess of W--------, who by repute would have four servants hold her spread-eagled on a great wooden block while a fifth and sixth used candles of impressive length and thickness to gradually cover her body with a coating of wax. This was apparently carried out three evenings a week in the great hall of her castle, with further huge candles burning in sconces around the walls and the moonlight playing upon her naked body from a high window. The process was said to take several hours, beginning with the application of wax to her least sensitive areas and culminating with her bosom and finally her private regions, which would induce erotic hysteria.

For those less well provided with servants and general facilities than the Countess, a simple household candle will suffice, although female kerilagniacs general prefer two or even three, so that once their arousal has reached a certain point the subsidiary ones may be put to other uses, marginally less peculiar but equally improper.

Whether this practice is to be considered an element of masochism, and those who enjoy inflicting it sadists, is open to debate, depending as it does on the heat of the wax as it strikes and the reaction of him or her whose skin it lands on. The above-mentioned Countess appears to have regarded the process as merely stimulating, and to have retained full control of the situation throughout. By contrast Miss L--- F------ prefers to have her naked posteriors simultaneously smacked and waxed, a somewhat messy process, and as her pleasure rises the candle must be brought closer to her flesh, resulting in a striking and undoubtedly masochistic condition of hysteria.

Klismolagnia

The practice of obtaining carnal pleasure from taking or being given enemas, in the masochistic form, or from administering enemas to others, in the sadistic form.

Here we may make an interesting contrast between, on the one hand, Dr J---H----- K-----, of Michigan in the United States of America, and, on the other hand, Madame F--- B-----, of Armentières in France. Both offer enemas as a service, both extol the virtues of this practice and recommend that copious volumes of water be utilised, and both employ young women in neatly starched uniforms to carry out the treatment. Furthermore, both employ clysopomps manufactured by M------ Frères of Lille in northern France for the purpose of administering their enemas. Only minor differences exist between their techniques, such as that while Madame B----- serves a glass of Champagne and a little *pâté de foie gras* on toast afterwards, Dr K------ serves yoghurt, half of which is eaten and the other half inserted into the bowel by means of a gigantic syringe. The great difference, however, is that whereas the good doctor is a respected medical man and vigorously opposes all carnal activity, expressing a particular abhorrence of onanism, Madame B----- runs a house of ill repute and encourages onanism as part of her treatment. Madame B-----'s establishment is also notably less expensive.

Madame B----- is a sadistic klismolagniac, and admits as much, if not in so many words, while her clients are masochistic klismolagniacs, or presumably they would not purchase her services. Dr K------, by contrast, is a man of utmost moral rectitude and a leading expert in nutrition, while his clients are earnest seekers after bodily wellbeing, which only goes to show how fine may be the distinction between the righteous and the depraved.

Kolpolagnia

A practice widely regarded as too lewd to exist outside the fevered imaginings of pornographers and the most crapulent of roués, and yet which not only exists but is regrettably common. Were this not the case, I would not trouble your sleep with such ignominy, but the harsh truth must be faced.

Without going into unnecessary detail, I can reveal that this practice is so widespread that it, or the desire for it, may be said to serve as the defining characteristic of lewdness in women. Those who are wanton crave it, those of a dominant or sadistic nature demand it, and those of sapphic appetite regard it much as you or I might regard partaking of a refreshing cup of tea. Indeed, my researches show beyond doubt that for women who have abandoned the righteous path it is this lewd and outrageous indulgence and not, as might be supposed, the insertion and vigorous movement of the virile member which provides the most felicitous and speediest route to erotic hysteria.

Nor is it always a simple matter completed in guilty haste or drunken forgetfulness. I have, on occasion, observed the practice to continue for over an hour, with pauses only for the occasional kiss or a sip of claret, and with a wide variety of subtleties and refinements employed. Such was the case in an incident between two of my maids, Miss F------ J---- and Miss L--- F------, not three weeks ago, which serves as the perfect illustration of this depravity. Both are, admittedly, fallen women rescued from the very slough of iniquity, and yet even I, inured though I am to every form of beastliness, could scarcely accept the evidence of my own eyes as they lay head to tail on Miss F------ J----'s bed. No detail was left unattended, including the posterior, an act I am still unable to bring to memory without feeling the need to lie down for a while.

You may be assured that this display strained my determination to maintain proper scientific detachment to the very limits. Nevertheless, it was not until their beastly lust had been consummated three and no fewer than seven times respectively, and my bottle of Château Grand-Puy-Ducasse 1868 drained to the dregs, that I intervened, calling both to my study for six of the best with a cane.

Kothornophilia

A condition in which footwear becomes the object of carnal desire, and unusual in being restricted almost exclusively to men.

There are no doubt as many types of kothornophiliac as there are types of footwear. However, it is possible to elucidate certain preferences: small size, a high heel, a pointed toe, the colour black, lacing, a high polish and in the case of boots a high reach. Hence my choice of term to describe this paraphilia, which is drawn from the distinctive heeled boots worn by tragic actors in the plays of Ancient Greece. Thus, while I have known enthusiasts, even fanatics, for scarlet silk ballet shoes, the Grecian toeless sandal and even clogs, the ideal of female footwear for the kothornophiliac may be presented as a thigh-high laced boot of highly polished black leather with a heel of six inches in height and encasing a slender leg and a dainty foot. It should be noted that while such a contrivance may delight the fetishist, it is far from practical and may indeed render the unfortunate lady unable to walk without extreme care.

So common is this beastly desire that a number of specialist cobblers exist dedicated solely to the supply of footwear for kothornophiliacs. In England alone there are three such firms, all located in the general area of Northampton as is the case with the shoe and boot trade in general, including Messrs H----- & C------, who must be regarded as the nonpareils of this curious profession. A further seven firms make lines clearly intended to excite the interest of the fetishist in addition to their normal produce. Other firms exist in France, Russia, Italy and the United States, but it is the Germans who seem most attracted to this particular depravity, with no fewer than seventeen firms employed solely in the production of kothornophiliac footwear, while it is a very inferior or else highly specialised German house of ill repute that does not offer this service. The city of Bremen, indeed, boasts three establishments that provide nothing else, including that of Frau S------------, where the girls wear thigh-length boots of exquisite manufacture and not a stitch besides.

It is curious to note that among the not infrequent lavenderists and rare sapphists who share this vice the preference is for rough, heavy footwear, such as might typically be worn by a quarryman or labourer, a taste in almost exact opposition to that prevalent among the majority.

Lactanolagnia

A depravity related to the drinking of milk, although not in the conventional manner, and associated with girls known as milkmaids, although not in the conventional sense. Rather, they are highly immoral strumpets who have little or nothing to do with cows, but who maintain themselves in milk not for the purpose of nourishing their offspring but in order to satisfy their carnal desires or those of their counterparts, the sucklers. This practice is as rare as it is beastly, so much so that when practised professionally the service commands a price higher than almost any other.

The typical milkmaid is a woman of buxom or even exaggerated figure, full at both bosom and hip, either matronly or, if youthful, exceptionally voluptuous. Milkmaids also, in my experience, tend to show a mild and giving nature, although I have been unable to ascertain whether this is because such character traits are truly typical or because such women are merely easier to corrupt.

Milkmaids are exclusively female, as to the best of my knowledge not even the most determined of transsexuals has managed to attain the impressive mammary development that goes hand in hand with this penchant, let alone bring himself into milk. Those who enjoy receiving milk may be either male or female, and, however beastly the practice, it is perhaps unsurprising that the need to suckle should apply to both sexes. Female sucklers tend to be of dainty proportion, and it is my theory that this is because they are unable to satisfy their urge upon themselves.

Surprisingly, given the extraordinary depravity of this habit, my notes reveal that a substantial proportion of practitioners show little or no shame. Lord and Lady R-------, for instance, are in the practice of taking their morning milk direct from their nursemaid, a woman of opulent charms named Miss F---- G-----. This, they claim, is done for reasons of health, the product offered by their local milkman, in Berkeley Square, being unwholesome owing to having suffered a long train journey.

I have observed this extraordinary display, discreetly hidden, and note that they feed together, direct from the teat, amid much giggling and teasing stimulation, which leads me to suspect that the nurse is in fact a milkmaid and that they are sucklers.

This fantasy also relates to cow-girls.

Lamechism

The practice of taking two or more wives, or simultaneous carnal partners in any measure.

While undoubtedly beastly this is a practice that appears to have met with acceptance and even approval during biblical times, which fact has been used as fuel by seducers, bigamists and others of disreputable habit. They argue that Lamech himself had two wives, Esau three, Abijah fourteen and Solomon as many as seven hundred, and that while this last case was clearly regarded as excessive, the sin of the last-mentioned was not having too many wives but allowing them to worship graven images. In any event, Solomon was duly punished by the fall of his dynasty, but Abijah seems to have suffered no ill effect at all, from which they conclude that a man may take at least fourteen women as carnal partners at any one time, a number sufficient to slake the lusts of all but the most greedy.

Pray be assured that the above reasoning is false, and that such ancient customs do not apply in modern times, especially in the case of rakes, scoundrels and philanderers who merely seek carnal gratification. By contrast, should a God-fearing and unmarried man take numerous women into his household for the purpose of shielding them from the wickedness of the world he need feel no more than ordinary guilt if from time to time his natural desires should get the better of him. In such circumstances I recommend an hour of prayer followed by an hour of vigorous exercise.

Lamiaphilia

A most dreadful form of beastliness, in that it relates to the eroticism of witches, witchcraft and all things pagan. Thus it goes beyond depravity to sacrilege, so much so that all those who practise it may be assured of eternal damnation.

As with so many beastly indulgences, the typical lamiaphile seeks to hide his or her depraved behaviour beneath a cloak of respectability, although as in this case that cloak involves not only heathen worship but Satanism itself, the word 'respectability' is hardly apt. A typical example is that society known as the Golden Dawn, whose very existence is a stain on the escutcheon of Christianity, old England and mankind in general. Founded by Mr W------ W------ and Mr S----- M------, and including in its membership Mr A------- C------, all degenerates of the worst sort, this group makes a variety of claims and conducts numerous rituals, none of which need concern us, for they are nothing but an excuse for orgies at which every imaginable depravity is conducted.

It may be that a proportion of such people are genuine lamiaphiles, although I suspect otherwise, but to my certain knowledge there do exist secretive and exclusively female orders who practise what may only be described as erotic witchcraft. While it is beyond my native ability to join such a group and discover the full truth behind such practices, I have on one occasion managed to observe a ritual which is in all probability not atypical of its type.

On the night of the twenty-first of September, 1875, while in the village of Chelwood Gate, Sussex, I chanced to observe a group of young ladies dressed entirely in black. Thinking that they were attending a funeral, I presented my condolences, but was more than a little taken aback by their giggling response. Most men would no doubt have put this down to bad taste, but I was by then sufficiently well versed in the depravities of the world to be suspicious of their intentions. I therefore kept an eye on them for the rest of the day, and with the fall of evening followed at a discreet distance as they made their way eastwards towards the Savernake Forest.

There they penetrated to a secluded glade and, beneath my astonished gaze, removed their garments in the entirety, each naked as the day she had been born, save only for their boots, which I imagine they kept on for practical purposes, the ground being somewhat rough. Thus attired, they set out candles placed atop goats' skulls and a wide variety of other paraphernalia, including thirteen enormous periapts, one to each girl. After the consumption of a considerable quantity of Port, drunk from an enormous chalice, the women then disported themselves in a circle, with hands linked, and began to dance and chant, spinning ever faster until they reached a state of dizzy hysteria. They then collapsed to the ground, seized their periapts, and with these and much work of tongues indulged in what is undoubtedly the most lascivious and unrestrained sapphic orgy I have ever witnessed.

So shocked was I by these events that I remained motionless throughout, and it was only after they had gone their way that I recovered sufficiently to regret not having done my duty by intervening in this ungodly ceremony.

Lavenderism

Carnal indulgence between men, a deplorable practice which must nevertheless be considered in some detail owing to its rising prevalence.

The country is, it seems, full of lavenderists, further evidence of decadence undoubtedly, but this is not the issue that concerns us here. Rather, we must ask ourselves: why lavenderism?

Whether one follows the accepted teachings of the theologians or that theory proposed by Mr C------ D-----, there would seem to be no space for lavenderism in the great scheme of things.

{Fig. 20} 'Some consider lavenderism to represent an æsthetic choice, arguing that the idealised male body represents the culmination of human beauty'

Some consider lavenderism to represent an æsthetic choice, arguing that the idealised male body represents the culmination of human beauty. However, as those who propose this theory are invariably lavenderists themselves, the argument is plainly circular and thus may be dismissed. A more tenable theory argues that it is the result of an excess of feminine influence from the mother while the child is in the womb, but this would account only for receptive lavenderists and therefore fails to meet the test.

Others contend that lavenderism is merely an expression of convenience, and that as a higher proportion of men are of depraved habit than women, it is easier for these men to indulge their beastly vices upon each other than upon women. This may apply to some extent to occasional lavenderists who also enjoy women, but otherwise is arrant nonsense. As any rake will tell you, it is the feminine virtues and physical delineations that provoke desire and the most beautiful boy is no substitute for the most homely girl. Besides, when one considers the low prices asked by ladies of negotiable virtue along the Whitechapel Road or even in Shepherds Market, this argument becomes ludicrous.

My own theory, which stands every test of logic, and also explains sapphism and the entire range of paraphilias, is that lavenderism represents neither more nor less than a diabolic influence, imposed upon mankind by Satan that he may seek to draw us into eternal damnation. *See fig. 20*

Ligolagnia

More generally known as bondage, this term refers to the application of physical restraint to the human body for purposes of carnality, generally by use of ropes. This must at first appear highly peculiar, given that one would have thought any person who had grown so debased as to give himself or herself over to the pleasures of the flesh would wish to remain unencumbered and thus allow the full expression of their depravity. There is, however, an explanation, which while superficially simple has required a great deal of research. It seems that being tied up has the effect of allowing one to absolve oneself of responsibility for one's conduct, and thus to engage in all manner of otherwise unthinkable acts. Ladies in particular seem to find themselves eager to make use of this excuse, and we therefore find that the majority of receptive ligolagniacs are female. Furthermore, their desires are generally expressed in the form of specific and frequently elaborate fantasies, of their own concoction, which must necessarily be carried out by a male companion.

The commonest, and simplest, of these is what may be loosely termed 'The Capture Fantasy', a mild form of zogreophilia. In this, the lady is pursued, caught and made helpless, usually by the simple process of tying her hands behind her back. Rendered incapable of resistance, she finds herself at the mercy of her captor, who indulges himself as he pleases. Thus she has gratified her carnal desires without surrendering her virtue, although in practice she no doubt knows perfectly well that her behaviour is an outrage to all that is decent.

An example of the above, and one which must also serve as a cautionary tale to the licentious, is provided by Lady M------- N-----. In order to enjoy her lewd proclivity for indulging two men simultaneously, she arranged that two local ne'er-do-wells, S------ T---- and J----- S----, should catch her bathing in a secluded pool on her husband's estate, bind her arms behind her back with stout cord, tie her ankles to ensure that she could not run, and, to quote the lady's husband, 'make thorough pigs of themselves with her'. Operations proceeded smoothly until the unexpected appearance of Lord N-----, his estate manager, his gamekeeper, two assistant gamekeepers, five men hired from the local village as beaters, and fourteen assorted guests who had come out to make up a shooting party. S------ T---- and J----- S---- fled the scene, but her ladyship, naturally, was unable to do so, and I regret to say that her husband's response was not a charitable one. He gave her over to the shooting party, not excluding the gamekeepers and beaters. This disgraceful episode, it must be pointed out, took place in the more ribald times of the Regency, and not recently.

{Fig. 21} 'I regret to say that her husband's response was not a charitable one'

Somewhat more elaborate is the desire to be tied into lewd and awkward positions, which, in its most evolved form, approaches the status of an art. Ligolagniacs both male and female indulge themselves in this practice, most often with the male doing the tying and the lady being tied. Competitions are even held, with a series of ladies displayed naked and bound in elaborate fashion, so that prizes may be awarded to whoever has managed to achieve the most æsthetically appealing effect, including considerations of the elegance of position in which the lady has been placed, the symmetry and pattern of the rope work, and the effectiveness of restraint. Curious though it may seem, these are usually rather restrained affairs (if I may be allowed a small pun), and only rarely do they descend into orgiastic practice.

We must also consider restraint as applied for purposes of flagellation. This is generally done with leather straps rather than ropes, and the primary purpose is to render the lady about to be flagellated helpless. Thus, it is said, her experience is enhanced, while it becomes easier for those who subject her to erotic chastisement to manipulate her clothing for exposure and apply hand or rod without fear of interference. My maid, Miss L--- F------, for instance, prefers her hands tied even if she is to receive a simple spanking. *See fig. 21*

M

Mackintosh Fetishism

Seldom, if ever, can a practical, sober invention have been put to such beastly uses as that patented by Mr C------ M--------- in 1823. Scarcely had the first of his long, waterproof coats been purchased than it was being put to improper use, as recorded in the case of Mr E------- M-------, who was apprehended in Sauchiehall Street, Glasgow, on the night of the twelfth of October, 1824, wearing a brand new Mackintosh, beneath which he was naked from waist to knees, with the lower parts of his trousers held to his legs by string. Thus attired, he had exposed his apparently ample genitalia to no fewer than twenty-seven women before being taken up by the watch. For this horrid crime he was transported to our Australian colony, which proved to be a mistake as he found the antipodean climate more conducive to his beastly hobby than that of his native Scotland.

Nor has Mr E------- M-------'s fate provided a salutary lesson to others. Since his day, the garment has become so popular among those who derive pleasure from exhibiting themselves to unsuspecting females that it may be regarded as *de rigueur*. Nor do such people have the shame and decency to restrict their habits to themselves, as my researches alone have uncovered three clandestine societies dedicated to self-exposure and the Mackintosh, one of which even goes so far as to issue a monthly pamphlet complete with anecdotes, humorous cartoons and advice to members as to the best locations, new techniques, the names of indulgent lawyers and more. *See fig. 22*

{Fig. 22} 'Scarcely had the first of his long, waterproof coats been purchased than it was being put to improper use'

Maid

A profession in which more young women have lost their virtue than any other, excepting only those that are openly disreputable such as thespianism and the circus. Indeed, so great is the risk of seduction for young girls in service that in my opinion they should, without exception, be obliged to wear chastity devices such as Messrs N----- and K---'s Protective Girdle in order to guard them against interference. It would also be a sensible precaution if the prettiest girls were only to be employed by men of the cloth and others of proven virtue.

Some may consider the above statement to show unnecessary alarm, but few have had the opportunities afforded to me by the nature of my research to make fully informed observations. I can therefore reveal a regrettable truth, which is that a substantial proportion of young men consider the household maids to be fair quarry for seduction, fornication and every type of beastliness, and, worse, that these attentions are all too frequently reciprocated. Indeed, I have known apparently respectable families in which maids have been carefully selected for their pretty faces, abundant charms and pliable dispositions specifically in order to provide the sons of the house with vicious entertainment and even worse. I shall give examples.

When Mrs R--- Y---- of Wolverhampton reached a certain age and her interest in the marital bed began to decline, she took into her employ a Miss F------ J----, a young, freckle-faced girl with an extraordinarily well developed bosom and an easy nature, specifically in order that Mr Y----'s attentions might be diverted from herself. In a similar but yet more depraved instance, Mrs A----- W---- of Lincoln took on two exceptionally pretty sisters, one, the plumper of the two, to take her place in coping with her husband's increasingly urgent præfocophilia, and the other to assuage her own sapphic appetites. I regret to say that both girls took to their new life with enthusiasm.

Furthermore, I estimate that in no fewer than forty-eight households out of a hundred the head of the family takes it upon himself to chastise his servants rather than leaving such, admittedly necessary, matters to his spouse. While the majority of such men no doubt start out with purely disciplinary intentions, it is not given to all to be able to resist having a warm, squirming girl held across one's lap with her bare posteriors reddening to the slaps of one's hand, and I fear that all too often this practice leads to improper behaviour: chirolagnia, irrumation and even proctism.

Such is the lot of the maid, and I have, over the years, made it my duty to rescue these unfortunate creatures whenever possible, to the extent which my income allows, sometimes employing as many as nine girls at once for a household that might do very well with two. Thus, in addition to my housemaid, Miss L--- F------, I currently employ five girls: Miss F--- L-------, whom I rescued from a flagellant house in Paris, Miss R------ W-----, who was formerly in the employ of the notorious apiolagniac Colonel Sir J--- C-----, Miss F------ J----, as mentioned above, Miss X----- M---, the daughter of a Chinese friend from my missionary days, and Miss S-------, whom I brought back from my last trip to Africa in order that I might save both her soul and her body, which is of proportions simply too tempting to allow her the company of ordinary men.

Mariscadoria

Not to be confused with an appreciation of small figs, from which succulent fruit the term derives, this is in fact the counterpoint to thyrsoadoria, but with the female organ substituted for the male. In terms of prevalence, I would rate the two practices approximately equal, but whereas thyrsoadoria is most commonly found among lavenderists, mariscadoria is rare among sapphists save for a single curious exception. There are also parallels in the favoured position, with the man inclined to kneel at his lady's feet so that he may indulge his passion, and in the tendency for practitioners to regard the object of their worship as of greater significance than all other considerations. Thus, a typical mariscadoriac, such as Mr A------ P------ of Middlesborough, will spend hours with brush and powder, sponge and eyebrow tweezers, as he brings that part of Mrs P------ to which he is so devoted to a state of perfection, although in all other matters he is a typical man of his class, preferring to put his feet up with a glass of stout than to assist his mate with even the heaviest of chores.

For sapphists, while their intimate parts are naturally the seat of their beastly indulgences, the term worship cannot normally be applied. They may worship each other, in a depraved variant upon the love normally found between man and woman, and they undoubtedly appreciate each other's physical attributes, but I have encountered only one form of true sapphic mariscadoria. This is one of singular depravity, and also both idolatrous and sacrilegious, for one of many disgraceful elements of the lamiaphiliac ritual described elsewhere in this text was the adulation of some imagined earth mother expressed by means of mariscadoriac kolpolagnia.

Masochism

A term derived from Mr L------ v-- S-------M----- (1836–95), which describes the practice of deriving carnal pleasure from physical or emotional mistreatment. Mr L------ v-- S-------M----- himself was apparently a man of somewhat specific tastes, but the term has come to be applied generically and embraces a wide variety of different types of beastliness, most of which are listed separately. Masochists are equally likely to be male or female.

Given their carnal tastes, one might expect masochists to be miserable creatures; physically frail, stunted in growth and of inferior natural characteristics in every aspect, also weak-minded, submissive in nature and lacking personal force. This is by no means always the case, and frequently the opposite is true. Mr G----- F--------,

{Fig. 23} 'A practice which might be excused on the grounds that
such rigours are a benefit to strength and stamina'

for example, achieved three gold medals at the recent Olympic games, but is known to train naked while being lashed across the buttocks and back by Mrs F--------, a practice which might be excused on the grounds that such rigours are a benefit to strength and stamina, were it not that while thus encouraging her husband the lady dresses in thigh-length boots of fine black leather, a fur coat and little else besides.

My personal theory is that such masochists feel the need to put aside life's cares and give themselves into the charge of another, although why this has to involve curious carnal practices remains a mystery. Equally peculiar is the division between physical and mental submission, which do not necessarily go hand in hand, as illustrated by Misses L------ and G------- P------, sisters, the elder of whom gains carnal satisfaction from the act of polishing their servants' boots but abhors pain in all forms, while the younger enjoys nothing more than to have her posteriors smacked by a strapping footman, whom she will instruct in exact detail throughout the process. *See fig. 23*

Mechaphilia

The love of mechanical objects or automata in preference to one's fellow human beings, and undoubtedly amongst the most peculiar of all carnal aberrations. Furthermore, my studies indicate that it is an almost exclusively female indulgence, receptive lavenderists excepted, although this may simply be a question of practicality. While having parts of mechanical contrivances thrust into one's body may be both ungodly and unwise, thrusting parts of one's body into mechanical contrivances is sheer idiocy.

I have noted only seven instances of this most peculiar of paraphilias, but one among them stands out as at once so grotesque, elaborate and ingenious that it puts all others to shame. This is the peculiar machine created by that most illustrious of engineers, Sir B------ I-----, to the order of his wife, that she might never want for

{Fig. 24} 'Nevertheless, its alarming aspect notwithstanding, the machine was apparently a success'

carnal satisfaction during his long absences from home. It is a squat, approximately humanoid construction of brass and mahogany, all finished to a fine standard and powered by a small, coal-burning steam turbine of a sort later adapted for Her Majesty's Royal Navy, but in this case the piston drives not a propeller but a rubberised priapt of such monstrous dimensions that one must fear for the lady's safety. Nevertheless, its alarming aspect notwithstanding, the machine was apparently a success, as may be judged by the continued happy marriage of Sir B------ I----- and his lady wife.

No successful male equivalent has come to my attention, although I know of three failed attempts, including that of Mr I-- M-----, who was second mate on an East Indiaman and would spend the long hours at sea attempting to perfect his machine. The consequences are said to have been disastrous.

Related to this are those machines designed to provide automated castigation. These are relatively common and can be remarkably ingenious, as is so often the case with depravity. The simplest of these employ the same principles as the bicycle, with the user perched on a saddle but with the system of chains and gears arranged so that the rotary motion drives an implement of chastisement repeatedly against his or her posteriors. I have known these devices to be constructed by flagellants either too shy, too cautious of their outward respectability or too smitten by guilt to follow the more usual channels towards their gratification, but they are most frequently found in houses of ill repute and used by clients with a girl in attendance. I have known similar devices to be powered by steam and, in recent years, by electricity, although these last are again notably hazardous. *See fig. 24*

Mesmerism

A normally harmless practice whereby a subject may be made to enter a trance-like state and so become subject to the commands of the practitioner. However,

{Fig. 25} 'A normally harmless practice whereby a subject may be made to enter a trance-like state'

I regret to say that I possess evidence of the abuse of this practice by persons intent on their own nefarious purposes.

Miss J----- D------, for example, was put into a trance by the mesmerist Dr I---- F------, his purported intent being to test her suitability as a stage assistant for his act. On being brought out of her trance, Miss D------ found that her clothes had been loosened and her corset retied with an unfamiliar knot, a situation that Dr F------ explained as being a common result of the powerful spiritual forces at work during the transition between the waking and trance states. Personally I have my doubts, but Miss D------ chose to accept his explanation and also employment as his assistant. *See fig. 25*

Missionary Work

In including this entry I do not wish to suggest that there is anything improper in the work of bringing God's word to the heathen, but rather to provide those intent on setting out upon this task with a forewarning of the temptations.

When I came down from Oxford in the year of 1845 it was my intention to spread the word to every far-flung corner of the Empire, and indeed beyond. I was confident, determined and, I now realise, somewhat naive. It was my belief that if there existed peoples who had yet to see the light it was only for want of opportunity, and that upon being presented with the incontestable and self-evident facts of Christian doctrine they would hurry to follow my torch. This proved to be an optimistic assessment, and, while I am not without my successes, my work did not go as easily as I had hoped, especially with respect to the teaching of higher moral values.

I had also seen certain pictures and been astonished to discover that there existed peoples so innocent of the principles of decency and decorum that they did not even wear clothes. It was these unfortunate souls who I felt would derive the most benefit from my ministrations, but as luck would have it the society with which I enrolled chose to send me to China, which had newly been opened to missionary endeavours. There I discovered a society very different to those I had imagined, primarily in that the natives, far from recognising the innate superiority of the English race, regarded us as barbarians. My task was therefore far from easy, and made harder still by the attentions of the local women, who were possessed of a strange and frequently intrusive fascination with the physical differences between themselves and Europeans. It is not easy to expound upon St Paul's letters to Timothy when a little Chinese strumpet clad only in a wisp of tight green silk is attempting to unbutton your fly.

In all I made three expeditions at various times in my career and in every case encountered similar temptations. Therefore I offer the following warnings to those who might wish to follow in my footsteps, and if I seem pessimistic then I can only plead the excuse of wishing to tell the unadorned truth. Primarily, the folk of much of the earth are as absolute in their various faiths as we are in our own, however mistaken this may be. Secondarily, the truth of the gospels is not as evident to heathens as one might hope, especially when they do not understand a word you are saying. Thirdly, women the world over have a fascination with that which is unusual, especially in male anatomy, and language provides no barriers to lewd desire.

Therefore, as you sit in a far foreign land, perhaps reading from the Bible to some dusky young maiden, do not be surprised if her hand should slip to the opening of your trousers, or if she should press herself against you. A man of God must accept these things and persevere, while doing his best to resist temptation, but should your flesh prove weak, reflect that you will not be the first to fail in this, nor the last. Furthermore, should you find yourself in a position in which some degree of acquiescence to immorality is required in order to continue one's work, it is better to do what must be done, and with a good grace. Remember, these things are sent to try us.

For example, you may recall seeing the obituary of the Reverend G----- M--------- in the *Church Times* some years ago, following a regrettable incident in British

Guyana, when he was cooked and eaten. I chanced to be in Demerara at the time, and it fell to my lot to go upcountry and remonstrate with the tribe in question for their ungodly act. This I did, praying hourly as I travelled and also fasting, although not, I confess, to enhance my spiritual qualities, but in the hope that a lean and bony figure might reduce their culinary avarice. Somewhat to my surprise, I was given a warm welcome, and a feast declared in my honour. You may imagine my trepidation as the cooks prepared their knives and assembled their ingredients, and since that night I have never been able to touch pork served roast from the spit.

Fortunately, thanks to the sterling efforts of my translator, I discovered the Reverend's mistake had been to offend the headman of the village by refusing the intimate company of his daughters. Thus, when he brought five giggling and partially naked girls before me I was able to behave with correct protocol, thereby saving my life and, more importantly, allowing me to continue my work. Indeed, I became greatly respected among the tribe, and a little wooden church now stands in the village, at the very spot where once a spit turned with its hideous cargo. Thus my choice is vindicated, although I confess that my outstanding success was in part due to difficulties in translation, as at the time I did not realise that to avoid giving offence I need only have accepted one of the girls rather than all five.

Mistress

A once respectable term now so badly corrupted by beastly use that the original has become all but obsolete. With respect to carnal practice there are two meanings, although they are not mutually exclusive.

Most commonly, a mistress describes the paramour of a rake or an adulterer, a woman kept in sinful luxury by some lecherous fellow that he may indulge himself upon her body at will in return for her continued comfort. While it is hardly surprising that such creatures belong to wealthy men, I regret to say that the habit is commoner among the aristocracy than among those who have made their own fortunes, and extends to the very highest in the land.

More rarely, a mistress is that lady who plays the sadist to a man of masochistic tendency, be it for her own satisfaction or for money, or both. Many a wife performs this function for her husband, and I have recorded a few cases of wealthy gentlemen employing a sadistic mistress for their personal gratification, generally in the guise of a governess or cook. Many larger houses of ill repute employ one or more sadistic mistresses to answer the needs of masochistic gentlemen, and some specialise in this function. Sadistic mistresses may also be of the sapphic habit, as exemplified by Miss E------ G------, who used to take a Mrs J---- W---- to bed for bouts of elaborate fornication involving a riding crop, several strings of amber beads and a small cactus while Mr J---- W---- remained bound and gagged in a convenient cupboard.

Muzzle

A device of restraint, consisting of a leather or metal cage fitted over the mouth parts and employed to prevent biting, casual ingestion or any other function for which the opening of the jaw is essential. Generally used to prevent dogs from seizing on their prey, the muzzle has proved irresistible to deviants, who use such devices as an element of bodily control, both for themselves and others.

Human muzzles are most frequently used for their own sake or as part of a more complicated system of bondage, the sensation being achieved by physical restraint and the consequent feelings of helplessness. I have found that physically powerful men of deviant character often enjoy being muzzled, but that women are seldom so restrained even by the most licentious of partners, possibly due to the inevitable restriction of access to the mouth. In the case of the other common usage of the muzzle, puppy-play, the opposite is true, and it is my experience that puppy-girls are made to wear muzzles as often as not, although so are puppy-boys.

In view of the great morphological differences between the human head and that of the dog or pig, muzzles cannot be adapted from those available for general purchase. The deviant is therefore forced to make his or her own device, which has led to the evolution of many extraordinary designs.

Nipiomimetophilia

The desire to be treated in the manner of an infant for purposes of carnal indulgence. First, it should be stressed that this has nothing whatsoever to do with actual infants, but is entirely an adult preoccupation.

There is a degree of association with bosom worship and suckling here, but while the nipiomimetophiliac is invariably a bosom worshipper and a suckler, the reverse is not necessarily true. Rather, the true nipiomimetophiliac is a specialist and an obsessive. Not for them the simplicity of a spanker or a stocking fetishist, who may indulge their beastly habits with little requirement for specialist equipment. To the contrary, for complete fulfilment of his or her penchant the nipiomimetophiliac requires a nursery, a nurse, a cot, a perambulator, swaddling clothes, toys, feeding bottles, teats and an extensive array of medical equipment, the exact nature of which it is probably best not to enquire into too closely.

These requirements make nipiomimetophilia very much a fetish for the rich, and indeed the idle rich, who have necessarily abandoned all vestiges of morality. Thus the successful, satisfied nipiomimetophiliac is rare, and is almost invariably an elderly gentleman of means so far gone in the ways of debauchery that he cares for nothing but his penchant. Such a one is Lord W---------, who, on the pretext of suffering from a range of unusual ailments, has not left the well-equipped nursery on the top floor of his Belgravia mansion for seventeen years, all the while attended by a succession of nurses whose sole duty has been to pander to his debauched whims.

Female nipiomimetophiliacs are rarer still, and I know of a single parallel to his Lordship, Miss L---- L-----, of Worcester, who plays the baby, and her companion, Miss F------- A----, who takes the role of nurse. Modesty has no meaning for the infant, and therefore Miss L----- will frequently find herself naked or, if not, dressed in elaborate and babyish clothes. She may expect to be suckled at her nurse's breast, fed by spoon, given a dummy to suck, bathed, dried and powdered, to have her most intimate parts inspected and her temperature taken by the insertion of a thermometer in the approved manner, to have her intimate parts rubbed with cream, and, most importantly, to be put in a nappy. Discipline seldom plays a major part in such scenarios, and for Miss L----- a firm spanking is generally considered sufficient. One might expect that for a grown woman to be so treated would provoke intense humiliation, erotic or otherwise, especially when her nappy needs to be changed or her bottom is spanked, but this is not the case. To the contrary, to Miss L----- the complete surrender of responsibility represented by her penchant produces a strong or even ecstatic sense of freedom. I have not been able to record the opinions of Miss F------- A----, but she appears to enjoy herself.

Nudophilia

Commonly known as 'naturism' or 'nudism', this describes the desire to be naked, and, most usually, naked in company, a beastly practice despite claims to the contrary. This is rare in our own country, but relatively common in Germany, from where the practice appears to be spreading.

Nudism is curious in that of all paraphilias its enthusiasts have made the greatest efforts to claim it as other than a carnal practice, citing benefits of health, a sense of freedom, and even that it encourages mutual respect, all in order to justify the indulgence of their desire. These claims are demonstrably false, but have been made so forcibly that I feel the need to demolish them one by one.

Health. Spend a day naked in the outdoors, even in our own mild and equable climate, and you are likely either to become chilled or to be burnt by the sun, while your skin will undoubtedly suffer from the attentions of insects and thorns, your feet from the sharp stones of the road and your dignity from the comic remarks of yokels. Nudity is not good for your health.

Freedom. Step naked into Piccadilly, St James Park or even the relatively undiscerning streets of some provincial town or village, and you may expect to be speedily arrested. Nudity does not confer freedom.

Respect. This is the most absurd suggestion of all. How is one to judge one's fellow man when he is naked, and thus to judge what degree of respect he deserves? Nor is there any relationship between pulchritude and worthiness; just the opposite. My own superior of the cloth, for instance, the Bishop of B---- and W-----, is a man who commands the utmost respect from all society, and yet he is elderly, heavy of body and possessed of pendulous jowls and a markedly rubicund countenance. If naked, how would one distinguish him from a retired stevedore, or indeed an unusually corpulent burglar?

As final proof of my assertion I offer the company selected by naturists. Frau F------, at her secluded park in rural Bavaria, invites many to share the supposedly health-giving benefits of her regime of outdoor nudity and bathing, but even a brief glance at the composition of her guest list will reveal that these may be easily divided into two groups, her own female friends of a certain age and wealth and youthful, pulchritudinous males. Search her male guests for spectacles, adenoids or a weak chin and you will search in vain, for to a man they might stand proud beside Narcissus or Adonis.

Nurse

A most worthy profession that for some reason proves an irresistible lure to rakes and men of depraved tastes. I have studied the reasons for this at some length, and conclude that it cannot be explained by one factor alone but is the result of several factors acting together. These are, in no particular order: the tendency of the profession to attract girls of a caring and unselfish nature, the relative independence of such girls, and the smart uniforms the girls are obliged to wear. It must be stressed

{Fig. 26} 'The senior Matron, Mrs L--- G-----, patrols the grounds nightly'

that the girls themselves are entirely innocent in this matter, but there is no doubt in my mind that it is a combination of these factors, and perhaps others, which produces so high a risk to a nurse's virtue.

An evening stroll past the rear premises of a hospital will reveal almost as many young men, and men not so young, with bunches of flowers or boxes of chocolates as one might expect to find outside the stage door of a theatre. These men, however, are not the ones who need concern us here, for their intentions, while not necessarily honourable, are seldom entirely beastly. Some may even be intent on respectable courtship.

Worse by far are the innumerable spectophiliacs, ostendophiliacs, klismolagniacs, omoiommorfophiliacs, flagellants and others who infest such places, seldom allowing themselves to be seen, for they know their guilt, but lurking in bushes or flitting from shadow to shadow, each intent on the indulgence of his beastly penchant. Fortunately, the authorities are well aware of this problem, and it is a rare hospital or nurses' home that is not well defended, although not infrequently the night watchmen employed for this purpose have themselves proved to be no less beastly than those they seek to guard against, or even in collusion. Thus we have the sordid case of Mr A----- M-----, who used to charge voyeurs three and sixpence to ascend the fire escape of the nurses' home he had been set to guard, or five and elevenpence ha'penny for added advice on which rooms housed the prettiest girls.

More effective guardianship is often provided by the matrons and sisters of the establishments in question, who tend to be robust women who stand no nonsense. It is, however, possible to take this too far. At St L---'s Hospital, Edinburgh, the senior Matron, Mrs L--- G-----, patrols the grounds nightly. She carries no lantern, but arms herself with a full-weight, three-tail, bull-hide tawse as manufactured by Mr J--- J D--- of nearby Lochgelly, a fearsome implement that she applies to the naked posteriors of any male she comes across without fear or favour. In her time she has spanked several quite innocent doctors, innumerable patients who were attempting convalescence, a variety of drivers, porters and so forth, and even her own brother, who had come to pay his respects on the occasion of her fiftieth birthday. All this might be excused if her efforts were efficacious, but they are not. She has, it is true, managed to rid the area of the usual deviants and also those young men intent on respectable courtship, but in their place she has drawn in a disproportionate number of masochists, and especially flagellant prægravophiliacs, for she weighs some twenty-five stone and is in the habit of sitting on the men's backs in order to ensure that they keep still during their spankings. *See fig. 26*

Nymphomania

An insatiable desire to reach, or approach, a condition of erotic hysteria. As this is, by definition, the diametric opposite of womanly virtue, it may come as a surprise for the reader to learn that the condition is associated with the fair sex rather than with men. The explanation for this, however, is that for the male the act of emission produces satiation, albeit sometimes brief, but this is not the case for the lascivious female, who, once she has broken free of the ordinary constraints of decency and prudence, may indulge herself until exhaustion robs her of her consciousness. Thus, true nymphomaniacs are invariably female, although I have known more than a few males who have done their very best to earn the title.

Miss L--- F------, whom I have taken under my own wing in order the better to study her condition, provides an excellent example of this disorder. Once aroused, no amount of stimulation will satisfy her need, nor repeated fits of erotic hysteria, nor any form of carnality, no matter how strenuous or bizarre. She will stop only when she faints, following which event she will sleep for as long as twenty-four hours without stirring.

Better known, although I would venture to suggest no less insatiable, was the notorious Comtesse d- l- R-----, who used to make it a point of honour to accommodate every single guest at the extravagant debauches she held in her château at St Georges-sur-Cher, be they men, women or otherwise. This she did not in the privacy of her chamber but on an enormous bed placed to one side of the grand salon, in full view of those awaiting their turn and those who had already been, breaking off only to take an occasional ortolan or a glass of Barsac, a combination she appears to have enjoyed almost as much as the indulgence of her body.

It would be a pleasure, at this juncture, to interpose a lesson on the costs of such flagrant debauchery, but I can not, in all good faith, do so. The Comtesse did not, as was regularly predicted, come to an early grave in consequence of her excesses, but survived each and every one of her detractors to pass away peacefully in her sleep at the age of one hundred and nine.

Obvolvophilia

The desire to be swathed in bandages after the fashion of an Egyptian mummy, which is peculiar enough in itself, and must be deemed doubly peculiar when done for the satisfaction of the carnal appetite. Nevertheless, obvolvophilia is not only a recorded phenomenon, but remarkably common.

Essentially, mummification is a specialised form of bondage in that it is designed to impose physical restraint upon the body, and yet it has curious and distinct features. Generally, those addicted to bondage ensure that certain parts of the body remain vulnerable, so that they may be interfered with according to the whims of whoever has tied them up. Obvolvophiliacs, by contrast, insist on complete enclosure of the body, thus rendering such intrusions impracticable. Also, while the art of bondage is noted for the multiplicity of positions into which the human form may be contorted and fixed, mummification is almost invariably carried out in a recumbent pose.

What then does the obvolvophiliac seek to achieve by his or her behaviour? As nearly as I am able to judge, the sense of enclosure is generally sufficient in itself and provides an almost exclusively mental stimulation, leading on to physical satisfaction only after release, although in some cases the body may be stimulated through the bandages or they may be slowly disarranged to maintain helplessness but allow access as the debauched scene rises to its climax.

The case of Dr T------ T------ of Rochester is typical and also instructive, as he became addicted to mummification after a long career as an Egyptologist, which provides clues to the disturbing and sepulchral thoughts associated with this practice. A less typical but equally peculiar case is that provided by Miss G---- S---, a nurse, who was found in her room wrapped from head to toe in bandages save for two small apertures, oral and posterior. She was adamant in refusing to confess the identity of her accomplice, and there was no evidence of intrusion to either the

{Fig. 27} 'What then does the obvolvophiliac seek to achieve by his or her behaviour?'

building or her person, which leads me to suspect some peculiar depravity of a sapphic nature. *See fig. 27*

⸻ ◆ ⸻

Omoiommorfophilia

⸻ ◆ ⸻

A somewhat unwieldy term meaning carnal delight in the wearing of a uniform, or in the observation of others in uniform. This is vulgarly termed 'uniform fetishism', which at least has the virtue of being easy to pronounce.

This common and varied paraphilia is found among both men and women in roughly equal proportions and is, in the main part, harmless. No overt indecency need be involved, and in ordinary circumstances one is inclined to be tolerant, such as in the case of women who find men in military uniform appealing. What, after all, could be more respectable than to show a preference for those gallant fellows who give themselves to the defence of our great nation by land and on the sea?

However, by no means all instances of uniform fetishism are so deserving of our indulgence. The habit of dressing up one's wife in a uniform to which she is not entitled, specifically for the purpose of enhancing erotic congress, must be seen as deplorable, and when the uniform in question is a mocking, eroticised parody of the real thing, more deplorable still. As an example, I cite the case of Mr S---- M----, who was in the habit of making his wife go about the house dressed in an approximate replica of that pure white uniform worn by Sisters at the nearby St T----'s Hospital, only with no undergarments save stockings and a skirt abbreviated beyond all decency, while she was obliged to wear the bodice unbuttoned, thus providing him with tantalising glimpses of both bosom and posteriors, which he would enjoy for a period of some hours, until, unable to restrain himself any longer, he would chase after her and perform the carnal act with her still in uniform.

This last point is essential to the understanding of this paraphilia. The omoiommorfophiliac has an active preference for the uniform itself, ideally with the lady in it, but the same lady in normal attire, or even stark naked, will not engage his interest at all, save as a desirable doll to be put in uniform. Thus we have the case of Lady G-------- G----, whose normal conduct was above reproach but who had an insatiable appetite for footmen, whom she would line up, sometimes a dozen at a time, all in full and correct uniform save for the exposure of their virile members. After a slow and extraordinarily lewd parade, she would give herself over to them on the floor of the hall, or on her front lawn if the weather was clement.

Onanism

The practice of self-stimulation, to the point of emission in men and erotic hysteria in women. I use the term advisedly, for while there is some debate on the exact nature of the sin for which Onan was struck down there can be little doubt that his hand came into play, even if only at the last moment.

This is undoubtedly the commonest of all carnal vices, among both men and women, and this despite warnings of the consequences from both men of the cloth and men of science. I can do no better than provide a quote from Sir W------ A----- (1857), who described the habitual onanist thus:

'The frame is stunted and weak, the muscles undeveloped, the eye is sunken and heavy, the complexion is sallow, pasty, or covered with spots of acne, the hands are damp and cold, and the skin moist. The boy shuns the society of others, creeps about alone, joins with repugnance in the amusements of his schoolfellows. He cannot look any one in the face, and becomes careless in dress and uncleanly in person. His intellect has become sluggish and enfeebled, and if his evil habits are persisted in, he may end in becoming a drivelling idiot or a peevish valetudinarian. Such boys are to be seen in all stages of degeneration, but what we have described is but the result towards which they are all tending.'

However, while few would dispute that this practice is inherently beastly, authorities differ as to what extent it represents a danger to physical health. In addition to Sir W------ A----- , numerous eminent physicians have stated that the practice gives rise to a wide variety of unpleasant symptoms, including blindness, mental deficiency, the growth of hair on the palms of the hands, and even premature death. Logically, one would expect to find oneself in agreement with such learned gentlemen, and indeed it is hardly conceivable that the Lord our God could allow such a beastly practice to be without consequence, and yet in the interests of scientific impartiality I must admit that my own extensive researches have so far failed to show that even daily onanistic practice is in any way deleterious to the health.

Sir W------ did not comment on the habit among women, and indeed appears to have been unaware of its existence. I regret to say that this is not the case, and that although the practice is clearly both beastly and unnecessary in the female it is regrettably common, also an important adjunct to erotic hysteria and nymphomania. Furthermore, it is deeply improper, especially for a lady of quality, and my advice for any man who catches a woman indulging herself in such a manner is to spank her soundly.

It should, however, be noted that the great majority of Englishwomen are quite unaware of such beastliness, especially as it pertains to themselves. For example, the case exists of Miss M--- P---------, who devoted the main part of her lifetime to the production of pamphlets dedicated to the suppression of vice among young girls, and onanism in particular. In evidence of the virtues of abstinence from this beastly practice, she would recommend her own robust health and comely appearance. She did indeed live to be one hundred and three, but it was only towards the end of her life that she discovered that the soothing nocturnal massage she had practised every single night since puberty was in fact the very act she had railed against so strongly.

Oplismophilia

Refers to a carnal delight in armaments or those bearing arms.
Some might argue that the general female appreciation of military men relates to this, but my own observations indicate that the desire is either for the native virility of fighting men or for their appearance in uniform and has little to do with the arms they bear, although I am prepared to grant that there may be exceptions, especially in the case of men with large swords.

Much commoner, although less explicable, is the male desire for women carrying arms, usually guns, which comes in two forms. Firstly, there is simple oplismolagnia, in which the gun is secondary. Lord G-----'s regiment of female soldiers were issued with the Brown Bess muskets typical of the period, but he appears to have done this for the sake of completion rather than in order to satisfy a specific paraphilia, although records suggest that he may have enjoyed interfering with the girls while they stood to attention, and subsequently giving punishment drill to those who dropped their muskets while being fondled.

Secondly, there is true oplismophilia, in which the gun becomes the primary focus of the man's beastly lust, generally for the power which it gives the object of his desire. Mr O--- E---- of Carmarthen provides a good example. A huge man, but of masochistic tendencies, he would only submit himself to his wife's sadistic ministrations if she was carrying a rifle and thus able to command real power over him by the threat of shooting him, which, unfortunately, she did.

Oppugnolagnia

Physical combat as employed for erotic purposes, generally wrestling or occasionally boxing, most often performed by women for the amusement of men, and all too frequently in a substrate of mud or some similarly glutinous substance.

In its simplest form this is a bucolic practice once common at fairs and in villages up and down the country, and also provided as a form of vulgar entertainment by troupes of itinerate buffoons. In the first case two local girls with a grudge might be put together in a ring, generally in a muddy field, there to take out their spite on each other. Apparently such matches almost invariably included vigorous attempts by each girl to remove the other's clothes and thus inflict humiliation. In the second case, the impresario or chief buffoon might either provide two girls to perform a staged match, with the first to be stripped naked declared the loser, or bring his own champion, who would strip and despoil the local girls for the amusement of the crowd.

Fortunately, such deplorable spectacles have long been banned in both England and Scotland, although it is my understanding that they occasionally occur to this day in remote Welsh valleys, conducted between the daughters of coal miners, who apparently wrestle in knee-deep slurry, often to the melodious accompaniment of the local male voice choir.

The practice is, however, alive and well among those private societies set up so that gentlemen of wealth may indulge their beastly habits in security and comfort. Thus, at the monthly dinner of the Birmingham Bacchanalians, a society composed largely of wealthy manufacturers of trinkets and cheap china ware, the tables are set out around a wrestling ring conventional in every aspect save that the mat is thickly coated in a mixture of mashed potatoes, mushy peas and black pudding. Girls are then invited to wrestle for purses of anything from five or six shillings to

{Fig. 28} 'Fortunately, such deplorable spectacles have long been banned in both England and Scotland'

several guineas, each bout being sponsored by one or another of the assembled industrialists. There is, apparently, no shortage of volunteers, despite the requirement for a win being for the victor to strip her opponent naked or to successfully conceal a black pudding in a fashion best left to the imagination. *See fig. 28*

Orgyism

The regrettable and sacrilegious practice of including more than two persons in a carnal act, although the term is more generally applied to events involving a large number of people.

Orgies are rare in this country, and even in the case of those societies dedicated to erotic indulgence the carnal act is generally performed in at least relative privacy. The Romans, Chinese and certain Indian cultures have all been noted for their orgiastic practices, and, not surprisingly, it is something generally associated with peoples of warmer climes and hotter blood. Exceptions, however, do exist, such as those parties reputedly held in the barracks of Lord G-----'s regiment of female soldiery, which, by all accounts, can fairly be described as sapphic orgies. Lamiaphiliacs also indulge in sapphic orgies.

Perhaps best known for their orgies were the inhabitants of ancient Babylon, whose licentious practices have long exercised the imaginations of romantic and erotic painters, who apparently think nothing of portraying several dozen scantily clad men and women, the latter notably more pulchritudinous than the former, and all manner of carnal behaviour, generally set in some great stone hall. How accurate these depictions are we cannot be sure, but all the acts I have seen depicted occur, even in our own society, and I therefore conclude that the primary requirement for orgyism is a complete and utter lack of shame.

An exception to this last rule is the masked ball, a curiosity of European origin particularly associated with the city of Venice. Here masks, often of great elaboration, are worn specifically in order to hide the identity of participants, so that they may indulge themselves without restraint in both adulterous and beastly behaviour.

Osphresiophilia

Obsessive erotic desire brought on by smells, pleasant or otherwise. This is a rare paraphilia, but interesting in that I am able to present a case study in which the origins of the condition are apparent.

For some years a Russian scientist, Dr I--- P-----, has been conducting experiments on dogs, by which he has shown that it is possible to cause a physical reflex, such as salivation in advance of feeding, by an unrelated stimulus, such as the ringing of a bell. It occurred to me that this might help to explain at least something of human erotic deviance, and I therefore set out to conduct a series of experiments of my own. These are still in progress, but I have already achieved a measure of success.

My maid, Miss L--- F------, whom I rescued from the consequences of her own nymphomania, provided the ideal subject for these experiments, although naturally they were undertaken in a spirit of strict scientific enquiry. She has a particular penchant for the cane, and has been known to reach a state of erotic hysteria through the application of that implement to her posteriors. I therefore ordered apple pie to be served at luncheon on a random selection of days across a three-month period, and, as the delicious scent wafted through the house, I would take Miss F------ to task for one matter or another and cane her soundly. On those days when apple pie was not served, I would leave her be. I then ceased to cane her for a period but continued to serve apple pie, and discovered that she now grew aroused by the scent of apple pie alone, even when she had been told that she would not be receiving the cane. This I regard as conclusive, and since the end of the experiment she cannot take so much as the merest whiff of apple pie without growing highly aroused. Thus she has now added osphresiophilia to her other vices, which must be regarded as an acceptable sacrifice in the name of science, especially as she is in my constant care and thus shielded from the dangers of the world.

Ostendophilia

The need to display oneself naked or partially naked in order to gain carnal arousal, commonly known as exhibitionism.

The exhibitionist is, in many ways, the natural complement to the spectophiliac, or voyeur, save in that such peeping creatures are generally male, while ostendophiliacs are female as often as not. Indeed, some aver that almost the entire female sex are exhibitionist, if only in a mild form. Personally, while in no way seeking to deny that women perhaps have something of a tendency to make a show of themselves, I do not think this can be classed as true exhibitionism unless it is deliberately erotic in nature. Thus, while the fine dress or expensive hat may well draw the interested attention of gentlemen, it is just as likely to be worn purely for self-indulgence, or most probably in an effort to incite jealousy among her less fortunate sisters.

Leaving aside the sordid machinations of the male ostendophiliac, let us consider the female. She is, in a sense, more fortunate than her male counterpart, for as she is expected to be more virtuous, so lapses in virtue are more readily put down to accident. Cunning is a crucial ingredient in her armoury, allowing her to make seemingly unintentional displays, from the minor, such as allowing a peep of a well-turned ankle as she lifts her skirts to avoid a puddle, to those which are a major outrage to public decency, and would be condemned as such did they not appear innocent. An instance of the latter is practised by Miss L--- H-------- of Eastbourne in Sussex, who, when bathing, contrives to allow the door of her machine to swing wide at an opportune moment, thus providing a brief glimpse of her naked body to a not insignificant proportion of those on the beach. Those wishing to remonstrate with Miss H-------- should note that so long as the weather is reasonably clement she bathes at three o'clock in the afternoon from Monday to Friday, and at both ten o'clock and five o'clock at the weekends.

P

Pachysarkophilia

The depraved desire for extreme bulk, usually in others and most frequently a male obsession. By this I do not mean a mild preference for voluptuous women, but a craving which can at times border on the maniacal and which can never truly be satisfied. There is no ideal for the true pachysarkophiliac. His motto would seem to be the more the merrier, and if his wife weighs fifteen stone and the opportunity to acquire a paramour of twenty stone presents itself he is likely to take it, and to abandon her for another of yet greater proportions in turn. The pachysarkophiliac is therefore likely to be an adulterous creature in addition to his principal depravity.

A peculiar and yet more monstrous variation of this paraphilia exists, in which one partner seeks to fatten the other up, as if she, or more rarely he, were a pig being made ready for market. This is extremely rare, I am glad to say, and should be distinguished from the principal form in that the fattener takes his pleasure not in his paramour being of ample proportions as such, but in the process of making those proportions more ample still.

My notebooks contain mention of over fifty examples of pachysarkophilia, but the most interesting among these is undoubtedly that of Lieutenant, later Rear Admiral, P------- W----- of HMS *Ravenous*, a frigate of thirty-eight guns, whose appetite for flesh appears to have known no bounds. Having spent some part of his duty patrolling the coasts of west Africa as part of the effort to stamp out the slave trade, he had learnt that the chiefs of some of the interior kingdoms prized large women above all else. He appears to have brooded upon this fact for some time, and to have tackled the slavers of the middle passage with extraordinary ferocity in his effort to find such a woman, free her and win her affection.

Despite winning numerous commendations, promotion and the thanks of Parliament he proved unsuccessful in his aim for seven long years, and his frustrations are recorded in the most vivid language in those of his personal logbooks I have in my possession. Finally he lost patience, assembled a shore party, cut his way through nearly a hundred miles of jungle, sacked three villages and brought away not one but fifty women, whom he describes as 'magnificent beyond all the bounties of Mammon'. He weighed each, and records in delight that not one tipped the scales at less than twenty stone.

In completing this foray he had also struck what proved to be a mortal blow at the local slave trade, and therefore returned to England to tumultuous acclaim, further honours and another promotion. He then retired, now a wealthy man owing to the booty he had gained in Africa, and, unable to choose between them, installed all fifty women as his maids and paramours in an elegant Georgian mansion just outside Bath, but died two years later of exhaustion.

Paddle

An implement of chastisement consisting of a flat piece of wood or reinforced leather with a handle, designed in such a manner as to make it appropriate for application to the posteriors. The paddle is more popular among our American cousins than within the British Isles or our Imperial colonies, and seems to attract an unusual degree of misuse.

Indeed, it would seem that among American students use of the paddle for ritual, comic or mildly erotic purposes has become so common that it may be regarded as *de rigueur*, while this sort of behaviour inevitably leads to its employment as an accessory to full-blown carnal indulgence among those of too weak a character to resist the effect. While the practice of 'hazing', whereby newcomers to academic establishments are obliged to receive a number of strokes with a paddle in order to gain social acceptance, is undoubtedly somewhat vulgar but not in itself harmful, the tendency to apply this to subsequent erotic encounters undoubtedly is.

{Fig. 29} 'Paddled by her maid each morning before breakfast'

Thus we have the regrettable example of Miss M------ H----, who chanced to attend an American college while her father was attached to our embassy in Washington, District of Columbia. At this institution she quickly gained new friends, and in order to be admitted to their sisterhood submitted herself to a ritual during which she was obliged to hold on to her ankles while her skirts and petticoats were raised and her drawers unbuttoned to expose her posteriors, to which a dozen firm strokes of a large wooden paddle were applied. Having gained acceptance to this exclusive society, she became an active participant in these rituals, applying the paddle herself on numerous occasions, until by the time she returned to England she had become thoroughly addicted to the practice, and now has her posteriors paddled by her maid each morning before breakfast. *See fig. 29*

Paliatsophilia

A peculiar affliction whereby the sufferer, and I use the word advisedly, is unable to attain carnal satisfaction unless dressed as a clown or, more frequently, unless the object of their affection is dressed as a clown. The same term may be applied to those who favour harlequinade or any other costume designed to appear ridiculous.

As is the case with many of the more obscure paraphilias, and indeed some of the common ones, the first instinct of the rational man might well be that anybody who does this should be safely locked away. I cannot agree with this attitude in general, as while to do this would be a wise and Christian act it would also rob of us of many of our leading politicians, military men and industrialists, with catastrophic consequences for the Empire. In the case of paliatsophiliacs, however, I would be prepared to make an exception, especially for those who do not dress up themselves but demand that others do so, a truly monstrous request, as evidenced by the case of Mr J---- T----- of Bolton in Lancashire.

Upon his retirement, having a made a fortune in jute, Mr T----- purchased an extensive, heavily wooded estate somewhat to the north of his native town. Here he took on a large staff, exclusively female and notably buxom, which he enlisted not from one or another of the respectable employment agencies available to him in the district but from houses of ill repute in Manchester, Liverpool, Leeds and other convenient cities. He also erected a high wall around his property and built a gatehouse in which he installed three retired prize-fighters in order to keep out the inquisitive. Thus he was able to oblige his unfortunate female employees to dress in a variety of costumes, united only by bright colour, ludicrous design and extreme abbreviation. Miss F------ J----, for example, who worked there as a scullery maid for a few months, was obliged to dress in a travesty of a mediæval jester's costume, patterned in red and yellow diamonds, skin tight from feet to throat, but with panels cut out to leave her bosom and posteriors exposed. Apparently the cook, a woman of matronly age and some twenty stone in weight, fared little better, but was at least excused the weekly 'hunt', during which Mr T----- would pursue the girls through his woods, indulging himself with whomsoever he happened to catch in the most beastly fashion.

Papilloadoria

The practice of treating the female bosom as an object of worship, which is among the commonest of depravities.

It is, no doubt, only to be expected that the female bosom should attract a degree of respectful attention from the male, for as God has seen fit to provide such bounties and man to provide clothing that enhances their natural magnificence, so admiration is not wholly unacceptable. Papilloadoria, however, goes far, far beyond mere admiration. A gentleman of propriety and breeding may allow himself a glance at a full bodice or a prettily displayed *décolletage*, but he will never make his

{Fig. 30} 'A gentleman of propriety and breeding may allow himself a
glance at a full bodice or a prettily displayed *décolletage*'

attention obvious, and much less make a remark upon the subject. By contrast, the papilloadoriac is unable to draw his eyes away, and will make conversation with his eyes fixed not upon the lady's face but upon that which he desires. Nor are his desires to be satisfied by what the lady chooses to display, as, if the opportunity presents itself, he will expose, fondle, squeeze, kiss, lick and smother his face between them, all the while engaged in furious onanistic agitation.

Perhaps unsurprisingly, for it is the bosom that nurtures all life, this practice has persisted throughout human history. In the very earliest civilisations it appears to have been the general habit for women to go bare-bosomed about their work, but in a warm climate and without the advantage of Christian teachings this is perhaps unsurprising and may have little to do with carnality. However, recent excavations at Knossos in Crete, initially by Mr M---- K----------- and subsequently by Sir A----- E----, and also at Akrotiri on the island of Thera, have revealed remarkable murals which show that the women of the time wore dresses cut so as to expose and enhance the entire bosom, in manner not at all dissimilar to the way open chemises are worn at establishments such as that of Madame F--- P----, at 56, Rue Fontaine, Paris. *See fig. 30*

Paraphilia

The generic term for any beastly habit which has become so strong a desire that it supersedes the procreative urge. Many paraphilias exist, and those detailed in this work should not be considered an exhaustive list. In theory it is possible to form a paraphiliac attachment to any object or concept, but in practice ninety-nine cases in the hundred are covered by those considered herein, excepting only a handful too abominable for inclusion even within the pages of this work.

The distinction should also be noted between a paraphiliac, for whom one or more depraved desires have grown to overwhelming urges, and the lagniac, who takes pleasure in many practices but shows no great preference for one over another and does not require a specific stimulus to become aroused. The true paraphiliac cannot achieve emission or erotic hysteria, depending on sex, without the stimulation of their penchant, whereas the lagniac may employ such depravities for the purposes of arousal prior to erotic congress, or as an accessory thereunto, and no doubt has preferences, but can manage without. In this work I have used one or the other suffix, according to the prevalence of philiacs or lagniacs associated with each specific form of beastliness, but with few exceptions it may be assumed that both exist.

Across the years I have encountered a great many rare paraphilias. These include: keraunophilia, referring to thunder and as exemplified by Major J--- F---------, who could only complete the act of erotic congress during thunderstorms and died when he was struck by lightning; nephophilia, referring to clouds, but not fog and therefore only achievable by ascent in a balloon, as demonstrated in 1892 by Miss F--- S-------; ornithophilia, referring to birds and leading to that unfortunate incident between Mr S-------- B---- and a wild ostrich; selenophilia, referring to the moon and illustrated by Miss O------ C----, who dares not go outside on moonlit nights for fear of an irresistible urge to remove her clothes; and xanthophilia, referring to the colour yellow, the condition that made Miss A----- C----- such easy prey for the Bengal Lancers.

Parthenophilia

An obsession with virginity, and as often related to jealousy and greed as to desire.

Virginity, and the physical expression thereof, is a gift given by God in order that a woman may bring herself pure to the marital bed, but it is all too often the cause of all manner of beastliness. At a simple level, the parthenophiliac desires virgins because they are virgins, at a conceptual level and in the same way as a chausophiliac desires stockings. The last thing such a person will do is to spoil the object of his affections, which can be most irksome for a young woman who marries such a man only to discover that he has no intention of consummating their union but expects his nightly satisfaction by means of epitrolagnia and onanism.

Rather commoner, and considerably more beastly, is the man who desires virgins because he relishes the act of defloration, and considers them soiled and of no further use to him after he has had his way. I have long made it my habit to horsewhip such scoundrels whenever convenient, and to take their unfortunate victims under my wing. There are also those who cannot bear the thought of any man having had carnal knowledge of a woman before himself, who are in a sense parthenophiliacs, although it is perfectly correct and understandable for a man to wish his wife to come to him as a virgin in proof of her virtue.

Next, we must consider those who seek out virginity as an expression of youth and beauty, a foolish and contrary view, for it is my experience that among any group of young men and women it is the fairest and freshest who are the most concupiscent and therefore least likely to be virginal. For some reason, perhaps fear of their own mortality and corporeal decay, this form of parthenophilia is notably common among the elderly, and although naturally this applies only to the debauched, they are not exclusively male. I would even go so far as to say that were one to make a study of seducers and their prey, the youth and beauty of the girls and boys would prove to be in direct proportion to the crapulence of the roués and harridans.

However, to assume that the beastliness must always lie only on the side of the roué or his female counterpart would be a grave error. Many is the unscrupulous fortune hunter who has presented himself, or more frequently herself, as an innocent in order to snare some wealthy but foolish victim, a ruse for which the parthenophiliac will inevitably fall. I, by the grace of God, am made of sterner stuff, and the last time some little strumpet attempted to lure me to the altar with the promise of her abundance I sent her on her way, with her bottom smacked but her virginity intact.

Pedisadoria

A practice in which the foot becomes the sole or primary focus of carnal desire. This is largely a male paraphilia, and for once this is easy to understand as it requires no great insight to appreciate the superiority of the dainty, elegant and unblemished female foot when compared with the outsized, calloused, hairy and reeking alternative presented by the male. Indeed, so one-sided is this paraphilia that whereas it is normally not especially difficult for the depraved man to find his lady counterpart, for pedisphiliacs the task is nigh on impossible. Few ladies, it seems, have more than a cursory interest in their feet, excepting only those who enjoy being tickled, and most grow quickly bored if their paramour fails to divert his attention to more promising parts of her body.

Thus the pedisphiliac finds himself in a difficult position, and, most often, resorts to employing a lady of negotiable virtue for the indulgence of his penchant. Indeed, so often is this the case, and pedisphilia so common, that in our larger cities specialist houses exist purely for the satisfaction of this depraved urge. There are two in London, one each in Glasgow and Edinburgh, three in Rome, and twenty-six in Paris. A typical example is the establishment of Madame F--- J------- at 35, Rue 22ème Février, where the gentleman caller on arrival enters a large salon to either side of which is a raised shelf equipped with chairs upholstered in rich blue velvet. On these chairs sit the girls of the establishment, each with her bare feet resting in a basin of scented water, from which she will extract them for inspection on demand.

For those pedisphiliacs who eschew base commercialism, or who are too poor or too mean to thus indulge themselves, the options are limited. The married man may be able to persuade his wife to assist him, while even a moderately wealthy man has the advantage of being able to select some pretty but guileless maid who may be cajoled or tricked into service, and indeed, so far is pedisphilia removed from the normal channels of erotic pleasure that it is sometimes possible for a man to fulfil

{Fig. 31} 'Mr A----- insists on measuring each customer's foot exactly'

his needs without the lady in question realising what he is up to. A case in point is that emporium of ladies' footwear run by Mr C------ A----- in the Brompton Road. Using his position as proprietor, and citing a quest for perfection as his reason, Mr A----- insists on measuring each customer's foot exactly, which, by my calculation, allows him to fondle over a thousand stocking-clad female feet each month. He also photographs choice examples, and his private albums leave no doubt whatsoever that he is no simple and honest perfectionist but a dedicated pedisphiliac. *See fig. 31*

Phobophilia

Carnal arousal through fear or, more pertinently, through deliberate exposure of oneself to fear. Thus we do not usually find phobophiliacs experiencing sudden carnal excitement due to some unexpected alarm, but deliberately placing themselves in a location or situation in which they expect to grow fearful and be able to indulge their beastly habit.

A good example of this is provided by Mr and Mrs W------- M----, confirmed phobophiliacs who have managed to make a partial profession of their penchant by accepting wagers as to whether they are capable of spending a full night alone in a house reputed to be haunted. I had long suspected that this practice was not entirely mercenary, and when they undertook to spend the night in W--------- C----, which is a strong contender for the title of England's most haunted house, I decided to observe their conduct. To this end I concealed myself in a large cupboard within the bedroom they proposed to occupy, and my suspicions were quickly confirmed, as with every creak or groan of the old house Mrs M---- would display increasing nervous excitement, until her husband took advantage of her condition. Their congress was of remarkable duration and also vigour, but unfortunately, in my efforts to make a full and proper observation of conditions, I dislodged a packet of elderly mothballs from a shelf within the cupboard, trod on some and fell forward into the room and on to the bed, causing the amorous couple perhaps a rather greater degree of fright than they had anticipated.

Pillory/Stocks

In common with the rack, these two mediaeval instruments of chastisement are not infrequently employed by the depraved that they may enhance their beastly indulgence. Nor does it appear to be sufficient for such people that the subject may be deprived of mobility and thus fondled at leisure. Instead, both stocks and pillory are most frequently employed in grotesque and lewd mimicry of their original punitive purposes.

A typical example is provided by Sir J----- F------, a Lancashire mill-owner who took to depraved practice only late in life and once he had grown wealthy, thus demonstrating the corrupting influence of money. Having purchased the manor in the village of Pitthorpe, Sir F------ proceeded to throw a series of debauched parties, which included several elaborate games, generally involving cards or dice and with the loser paying a forfeit of an erotic nature. On one such occasion Sir F------ himself lost the game and was duly taken down to the old village pillory and fastened into place by his drunken friends, both male and female. Thus secured, he was pelted with tomatoes, eggs and other traditional substances, following which treatment one of the ladies present adjusted his lower clothing and performed an immoral act upon him, to the loud approval of the audience. So great was the noise that the local constable was roused from his bed and the revellers fled, all save Sir F------ himself, as in their drunken haste his associates had brought a padlock but no key.

Podoadoria

An obsessive desire associated with legs, and almost invariably with ladies' legs, for in ninety-two cases of a hundred the podophiliac is male, and in the remaining eight is a female of sapphic preference.

The typical podophiliac is a sorry fellow, nervous of disposition and with a distinctive crick to his neck, both factors which result from the difficulty of satisfying his penchant, for whereas for the bosom-lover ladies carry their glories before them, and for the fundoadoriac the effects of corsets and the cut of dresses are at the least designed to spark his imagination, for the leg-lover there is no such resource. Therefore we find him constantly peering sideways in the hope of catching a glimpse of ankle or calf, which accounts for the peculiar angle of his head, and of a nervous disposition due to the constant risk of finding himself accosted by either a lady who has noticed the lewd quality of his attention or a member of Her Majesty's Constabulary.

However, if the podophiliac is successful in a seduction, marries a wife of less than stringent morals or consorts with ladies of negotiable virtue, he is at least likely to find his desire appreciated, unlike those whose beastly lusts are focused on feet or shoes. As even the apprentice rake soon discovers, ladies' legs are sensitive to the touch. Thus, if her morals are not too high and her general interest is aroused, caresses to her legs form the surest route to yet more intimate areas. Many a first exploratory caress has been applied to the leg, and once the podophiliac has his lady friend stripped down, he may indulge his penchant at leisure, confident in his knowledge that no matter how long he takes at kissing and caressing her calves and thighs she is unlikely to grow bored.

As with many paraphiliacs, the podophiliac has certain distinct preferences when it comes to the female form. Where the prægravophiliac prefers the ample figure and the papilloadoriac a tiny waist and a voluptuous bosom, the podophiliac appreciates

{Fig. 32} 'She may feast her eyes on that which she desires in a broad variety of circumstances without arousing suspicion or condemnation, so long as she places herself in the right surroundings'

height and elegance, ensuring that the ladies' legs are as long and as shapely as possible. He is also likely to be inclined to chausophilia, and to take particular enjoyment in smooth, unblemished skin.

His sapphic counterpart is more fortunate than the male podophiliac, in that she may feast her eyes on that which she desires in a broad variety of circumstances without arousing suspicion or condemnation, so long as she places herself in the right surroundings. Thus we have the curious case of C-------, Lady B----------, a young woman of ample fortune who nevertheless took employment as lady's maid with a family called B----, tripe merchants of Salford in Lancashire, a most peculiar choice until we consider that the household of Mr B---- included his wife, her two maiden sisters and five daughters, all tall shapely girls with exceptionally well formed legs, and that Lady B----------, a podophiliac among podophiliacs, was required to assist all eight women with their stockings and garters each morning. *See fig. 32*

Ponolagnia

Is the practice of taking an immoral relish in painful stimulation. This must be distinguished from masochism in that a ponolagniac enjoys pain for its own sake rather than as an element of submission or humiliation.

Ponolagnia may be associated with a particular fetish, such as trampling or agitation of the teats, but in its pure form the pain may be inflicted by any convenient means, and indeed it is most often a solitary pursuit. In a typical case, let us say with a female ponolagniac such as Miss G------ S----- of Putney, she will choose a quiet moment and a secure place, disrobe and disport herself in an appropriate position. Initially, she will pinch the flesh of her breasts, belly and thighs, thus slowly building up her arousal and need. Once her passion is inflamed, she will typically substitute for her fingers an implement such as a stiff hairbrush or, not infrequently, a Wartenberg pinwheel, a medical device designed to test the neurological reactions of a patient's skin, which is, apparently, most effective for inducing mild pain. As a serious addict to this form of beastliness, she may then progress to needles, clamps designed to pinch the flesh of her teats and other intimate parts, or any other instrument she finds effective, stimulating herself until at last she can hold back no more and is forced to bring herself to a condition of erotic hysteria.

Præfocophilia

Technically, this beastly paraphilia involves the pressing of any fleshy part of the corpus to the mouth for the purpose of increasing carnal desire by restriction of breath, and may be indulged between any two people. In practice, the fleshy parts in question are almost invariably the posteriors or bosom of a woman and in more than nine cases out of ten the receptive præfocophiliac is a man.

The essence of præfocophilia is that the lady involved should be of ample development and, within reason, the more ample the better. This is logical, however depraved the reasoning which leads to such a conclusion may be, as the larger the bosom and posteriors of the lady in question, the more effectively she can carry out her allotted task. It is, perhaps, also understandable that those women who enjoy smothering a lover tend to be ample, and this is undoubtedly the case, as their more slender sisters may find their natural physical attributes inadequate to the task.

What is less clear is why male enthusiasts for this vice are almost invariably dainty or even wizened. When measuring præfocophiliacs I have discovered the males to have an average height of five feet and four inches, combined with a weight of eight stone and four pounds, both well below the average figure. Their female counterparts, by contrast, were above average for both height and weight, respectively five feet eight inches and thirteen stone for those engaged in the indulgence of their own vice, and, for those coerced into it by one means or another, no less than five feet eleven inches and twenty-four stone three pounds, although for a lady of such dimensions, 'coerced' is perhaps not the *mot juste*.

Prægravophilia

The practice of taking pleasure in exerting one's weight upon another, or in having the weight of another exerted upon oneself as if being squashed. As with the related practice of præfocophilia, the giving participant is generally female and the receptive participant male, while there are also parallels in that women who thus indulge themselves are generally large and those who are coerced into such indulgence larger still, the average of this last group reaching an astonishing twenty-five stone and four pounds. Male prægravophiliacs, however, are not unusually small, which in the circumstances is probably just as well.

As is common with the less overtly carnal paraphilias, prægravophiliacs frequently disguise their beastly lusts as something else, usually of a medical nature. Thus Sir L----- H----- QC, claiming the advice of his physician, employed only the most ample of female staff and demanded that they sit on him twice daily, in strict rotation between the chambermaid (who weighed eighteen stone six), the cook (who measured an impressive twenty-one stone four) and the dairymaid (at a frankly extraordinary thirty stone and one pound). It should also be noted that despite his peculiar habits, competition was always keen to win employment with Sir L-----, whose servants' table had the reputation as the most generous in the county. *See fig. 33*

{Fig. 33} 'It should also be noted that despite his peculiar habits, competition
was always keen to win employment with Sir L-----'

Priapt

An instrument designed to mimic or replace the virile member, as utilised by nymphomaniacs, those of the sapphic persuasion and a number of physicians.

Curiously, this depraved device casts light on humanity itself. The typical priapt is carved in more or less accurate imitation of the member it is intended to replace and also has certain inevitable dimensions, being, on average, approximately one-third again larger than the average for the human member estimated by Dr E------ B----- in 1862. Thus there can be no mistaking the ancient priapt when it is discovered, as it has been in deposits and burial sites from the Palæolithic onwards, proving that female depravity is not, as some claim, a product of contemporary social decay but has been with us since time immemorial.

However, the researcher or collector of curios should beware of rogues, notably in Egypt. A number of Egyptian priapts have been found, the oldest of these predating the first dynasty, but these are far outnumbered by fake items on offer in the markets of Cairo. I personally have been offered no fewer than seven priapts in the course of one afternoon, all of which were supposed to have been the personal property of Queen Cleopatra.

I have seen priapts made of stone, wood, ivory, even malachite and lapis lazuli, but in recent years rubber has become the material of choice and is, it would seem, a versatile and efficacious material for this purpose. Indeed, Messrs B--- and H-------- of Birmingham have recently added to their normal range of tyres, gaskets and tubing a selection of three priapts, the small 'Percy' of six inches in length and five in girth, the medium 'Anstruther' of nine inches in length and seven in girth and the large 'Goliath' of a full foot in length and nine inches in girth. This last is an object so disproportionately grotesque that any well-bred lady would undoubtedly faint at the mere sight of one.

The priapt is also the instrument of choice among those physicians who believe that ordinary feminine hysteria may be relieved by bringing the patient to a condition of erotic hysteria. The principal proponent of this somewhat suspect theory is Dr E---- v-- H----- of Rotterdam, who uses a large rubber priapt to effect this procedure. While I have my doubts as to his motives, it must be admitted that, at least on those occasions when I have been present, the technique appears remarkably efficacious. However, the treatment takes some time, and following certain observations of a lewd young girl seated on a pumping apparatus and his own experiments with electrostimulation, he theorises that better results might be obtained if it were possible to somehow insert a small electrical engine within the priapt, thus causing a vibration of high frequency such as the girl on the pump was employing for her satisfaction. He may well be correct, but with those electrical engines currently available the resulting priapt would have to be some eighteen inches in diameter, which I feel is unfeasibly large.

Proctism

A most base depravity in which the virile member is introduced not where nature intended but in close proximity thereto, between the posteriors. Please note that proctism should not be confused with that practice for which God destroyed the ancient city of Sodom, which involves the insertion of the virile member into any convenient receptacle saving only that for which it was intended. Although unthinkable to all decent persons no matter what the provocation, proctism is a common practice and is carried out for a wide variety of reasons, all of them thoroughly immoral.

I have discussed this subject at length with Madame F--- M-----, whose establishment at 21, Rue de Tours in Orléans specialises in all matters of carnal gratification as it relates to the female posteriors. She theorises that men are easily overcome by the glory of this particular aspect of God's creation and that proctism, while essentially mistaken, is therefore an understandable culmination of conventional desire. Others, she states, are so poorly endowed by nature that normal congress is unsatisfactory, while a significant minority indulge in the practice precisely because it is so unutterably beastly. This last excuse, having met some of her clients, I can well believe.

Still others excuse their behaviour on the grounds of wishing to avoid procreation, apparently oblivious to the fact that this is the exact purpose for which man and woman are gifted to receive carnal pleasure. More peculiar still, if perhaps less beastly, are those who view proctism as a form of abstinence. Mr J--- H------- of Southwold in the county of Suffolk, for example, is in all other ways a respectable married man, and notably pious, yet every Sunday he refuses to address himself to his wife in the normal fashion and inserts himself between her posteriors instead. He also does this for the entire period of Lent.

Lavenderists claim that they have no alternative to proctism, but this argument is plainly specious. Does the desire for a succulent cutlet or a prime cut from a rib of beef excuse cannibalism? It does not, and even if we accept my theory that lavenderism is a diabolic influence over which we have little control, this does not excuse proctism. Far better, surely, to take a cold shower followed by a period of quiet prayer, or, if they are truly incapable of controlling their base urges, a session of mutual chirolagnia or even exchanged irrumation would be preferable to this blackest of deeds. Erotoaplistiacs use the same excuse but with even less justification, and least excusable of all are those men who enjoy the practice at the hands of a sadistic woman with a priapt.

For women and men, even the most rampant of lavenderists, to enjoy being on the receiving end of this practice must surely be due to diabolic influence, for they plainly do enjoy it, and who else but Satan could craft so cruel and lewd a joke upon mankind?

Quean

A colloquial term for a lavenderist of distinctive character. Whereas such men are usually at pains to hide their personal proclivities, the quean struts abroad as if he had nothing to be ashamed of, head held high and dressed in as extravagant a fashion as his purse will allow. A taste for flamboyant waistcoats and voluminous cravats is typical of the quean, and he may be distinguished from more conventional dandies by his choice of colour for these clothes, most frequently lilac, apricot or pink.

Undoubtedly the most notorious quean of recent years is Mr O---- W----, whose scandalous career came to an end following his unsuccessful attempt to sue the Marquess of Q---------- for libel. Thus pride comes before a fall, a lesson from which we all can benefit, although one might argue that in this case Mr W---- was guilty not so much of pride but sheer folly, for he was a familiar sight to those of us who frequent the Piccadilly and Soho districts of London, for whatever reason, and as often as not he was to be seen in company with young lavenderists whose affections were well known to be both accommodating and negotiable. *See fig. 34*

{Fig. 34} 'Mr O---- W----'

Queening

An expression in scandalously poor taste, as it is apparently derived from the upright fashion in which our glorious monarch sits her throne, which has come to be used by those of depraved character for the way in which a woman sits atop a gentleman's face in order that he may perform a lewd act. Astonishing though it may seem that any man can so sacrifice his dignity as to allow a woman to use his face as a seat, or that any woman might wish the extraordinary familiarity and exposure involved in thus seating herself, this is a remarkably common aberration. Furthermore, the practice is almost always carried out with the lady's drawers open and her posteriors bare, creating an intimacy of contact which decent people may find it hard to conceive.

In the course of my researches I have seen this done with remarkable frequency, and not merely in the houses of ill repute to which one might hope such things would be confined. To the contrary, while no doubt in the majority of cases the queen is a lady of easy virtue and her mount a gentleman of depraved habit who has paid for his penchant to be realised, I have witnessed this extraordinary conduct between many apparently respectable people, including a man and his wife, a young sailor and his sweetheart, and a butler with a cook of such voluptuous charms that it is a surprise the fellow was not suffocated.

Perhaps most extraordinary of all was the case of two young ladies on a hot summer's day beside the River Cherwell. These were students of the nearby S--------- College, whom one might suppose and hope to be models of intellectualism, restraint and propriety, and yet I personally observed them to take turns in seating themselves upon each other's face. This was done with their drawers parted and their skirts and petticoats spread out like great colourful flowers, so that in each case their companion's booted feet protruded from beneath. In this fashion they reduced one another to a state of giggling hysterics by the application of their

{Fig. 35} 'Students of the nearby S--------- College, whom one might suppose
and hope to be models of intellectualism, restraint and propriety'

tongues to each other's nether regions; and all the while whoever was mounted upon the other paused occasionally from the indulgence of her vice to enjoy a slice from a large pie, game I think. *See fig. 35*

Quirt

A short, flexible whip made of plaited leather and generally with a twin-tailed sting. This is a favoured implement among the depraved as it may be carried with all innocence, is too light to risk damage even to tender female posteriors, and yet produces a sharp and effective stinging sensation of the type widely favoured among flagellants.

In the nature of such an implement, the quirt may be used by any person of sufficiently depraved nature to wish to do so, but I have found it notably favoured by two groups: the drivers of London Hackney carriages and those who habitually ride to hounds. In the former case a typical example is provided by the enterprising if beastly J--- S----, a cabman who used to offer a dozen light strokes of the quirt to chorus girls and so forth, that they might find it easier to cope with the demands of those elderly roués who had paid for their services. For this he would charge sixpence in addition to his normal fare.

The latter case is best illustrated by Mrs V----- J------, who was notorious for enjoying the application of a quirt to her naked posteriors after a day's hunting. So shameless was she that not only did she on occasion demand this service from her grooms rather than her lawfully wedded husband, but she seldom troubled to wait until she could retire, preferring to be whipped in the stable yard among the horses and hounds.

R

Rack

A mediæval device of torture sometimes corrupted, albeit rather inefficiently, to carnal use.

There is, in fact, only limited similarity between the original and its modern counterpart. The mediaeval version was a great wooden slab fixed with heavy chains and a wheel-and-ratchet device capable of exerting lethal pressure. A typical erotic version, by contrast, is smaller, of less robust construction in general, fitted with light and elegant fetters and, generally, padded, while the wheel-and-ratchet system exerts only sufficient pressure to hold the subject immobile so that he or she can be subjected to erotic torments at leisure, perhaps tickling, spanking or the application of hot wax. Indeed, in many continental houses of ill repute the 'rack' proves to be no more than a bed fitted with light, padded fetters and some simple device for tightening these, yet more evidence of the soft and decadent nature of both deviants and foreigners.

The Englishman is of sterner character, and that rack displayed in the Yorkshire dungeon of Sir J--- M---- at least approximates to the original. However, the Scot appears to be sterner still, and I have observed one genuine instrument in use, that employed by Lord F--- in his ancestral seat on the island of Benbecula. A large and powerful man of exceptionally robust character, he took his pleasure in ways that would have been impossible for lesser men. His particular penchant was to be racked by his wife and female servants, who would simultaneously apply an enormous four-tailed tawse to his strong and hirsute posteriors and manipulate his virile member. Lord F--- never seemed to suffer ill effects from this treatment, although it is possible that his height might have been rather less impressive had be spent less time being stretched; but the same cannot be said for the rack. Originally built in 1504, this great machine proved to have rotted right through and finally collapsed during a particularly strenuous set of erotic exercises, during which her Ladyship was mounted on the Lord while he was simultaneously queened by the cook.

Rahabism

The practice of accepting payment, in whatever form, for carnal satisfaction, which may be included among those indulgences which are now considered immoral but in early biblical times were not.

Leaving aside the motives of Rahab herself, which were far from simple and appear to have been motivated principally by a perhaps understandable desire not to be struck down, it is quite evident that no blame whatsoever attaches to the two Israelites who spent the night with her. Indeed, the issue is not even remarked upon. Equally, Judah seems to have considered it perfectly ordinary to offer a woman he met at the roadside a young goat in exchange for erotic congress. Judah was a cautious man, as we know from his treatment of Joseph, and at this time two of his sons had already been struck down for sinful practice, so he was quite evidently confident in his safety. He also appears to have had no qualms about indulging himself beside the road, but he was a herdsman and so we may put this down to his rustic nature.

Nor do the strictures of Leviticus apply to rahabism itself, but to specific usages involving priests and the daughters of priests. Hosea and Micah were rather more disapproving, but again in distinctly unusual circumstances. It is only much later that the practice is regarded as openly sinful, and even then to state that it is beyond redemption is to fly in the face of the highest authority, our Lord himself. I therefore conclude that rahabism is both beastly and sinful, but only moderately so when considered beside practices such as sadism or klismolagnia.

Reiphilia

The desire to view another not as a fellow human being, but as an object, and, specifically, an eroticised object. Thus, for the male reiphiliac a woman becomes a collection of visually pleasing parts, hair, face, bosom, waist, posterior, legs and so forth, or for many fetishists a pretty vehicle for the true object of his affections, which might be her shoes, drawers or corset, or even some more abstract quality such as her weight or the haughtiness of her glance. Equivalent concepts apply no less to the female reiphiliac.

Certain authorities hold that this is not a valid concept at all, but merely a means of expression whereby it is easier for the paraphiliac to see others in terms of their personal penchants rather than as fellow human beings. I disagree. The typical paraphiliac is quite capable of seeing others as they are, and indeed almost invariably he or she will go to enormous efforts to seek out those with compatible tastes.

True reiphilia is something different entirely, and relates to agalmatophilia, only instead of wanting a statue as a partner, or a partner willing to imitate a statue, the reiphiliac wants him or her to be lacking in all personal volition. Thus, the true reiphiliac desires absolute, unprotesting compliance on the part of his or her partner, so they may do exactly as they wish and have exactly what they wish done to them in return.

In the course of my researches I have come across a number of reiphiliacs, both male and female, and have reached the conclusion that their paraphilia is neither more nor less than extreme selfishness. By contrast, while I have come upon many whose dearest wish is to be enslaved, tied helpless or flagellated, I have yet to find a single person who genuinely wishes to relinquish their control and become purely the object of another's pleasure without reference to their own, despite claims to the contrary.

For instance, the noted reiphiliac Mr O------ F--, of Parsons Green, claimed for many years that his wife was so utterly devoted to him that she had become to all intents and purposes an object existing purely for his pleasure, until one night, after an especially elaborate erotic engagement, he declared his intention of going to sleep before she had reached a condition of erotic hysteria, upon which she broke a chamberpot over his head and expelled him from the room and house with blows, profane remarks and the assistance of a small japanned statue of Salome dancing before Herod, which they had been using to assist in their congress.

Rubber Fetishism

An unhealthy carnal obsession with rubber and, more specifically, with the properties thereof.

It is seldom if ever sufficient for a rubber fetishist to simply handle a piece of rubber in the way a stocking fetishist might handle a pair of stockings. Rather he or she must envelop themselves in the material, sometimes simply by rolling themselves up in it, but more frequently by using it to make clothes. With sufficient determination, and determination is something that the depraved seem to possess in abundance when it comes to indulging their penchants, it is apparently possible to imitate any article of clothing in rubber, but much the most popular are undergarments. Thus we most often find the male rubberist in a pair of tight longjohns, while the female enjoys far greater elaboration.

Mlle F--- B-----, of Poitiers in central France, for example, wears rubber from head to toe, including stockings, a pair of drawers so tight that they reveal every exact contour of the flesh beneath, a little skirt resembling a greatly abbreviated petticoat, flounced at the edges and too short even to fully cover her posteriors, a corset, boned and studded, a chemise no less tight nor less revealing than her drawers, long black gloves and a curious hood, from the top of which her hair projects as if it were the tail of a horse. Only her shoulders, the lower part of her face and her eyes remain exposed, and while her drawers do indeed split in the normal manner, this is purely in order to enable her to properly entertain her numerous clients. *See fig. 36*

{Fig. 36} 'While the female enjoys far greater elaboration'

S

Sadism

The practice of taking pleasure in the physical or emotional mistreatment of others, the counterpoint to masochism, and likewise named after a noted practitioner of the vice, in this case Comte D-------- A------- F------- d- S---, a notorious French libertine and flagellant, commonly known as the M------ d- S---, although it should be noted that his depravities varied only from those of his fellow countrymen in that he was in the habit of writing them down.

Some authorities consider that a necessary prerequisite of sadism is that the object of the cruel lust should be unwilling to bear it, but my own, extensive, research shows that for all practical purposes the opposite is true. In order to give full rein to his beastliness, the sadist requires a willing partner, one who will not only accept whatever torments are inflicted but will be grateful and respond with grovelling servility. The reason for this is that extravagant vanity and a bloated self-esteem go hand in hand with this vice, as Stilton cheese goes hand in hand with crusted Port.

An example, and a disgrace to the good name of English nobility, is the Lady M------ B--------, who in the course of a long and pampered life has seen fit to gather around herself an entourage of men and women who are to all intents and purposes her willing slaves. These include her husband, numerous paramours and a full complement of servants, upon whom she inflicts the most extraordinary range of cruelties and humiliations, including having her carriage pulled by a team of no fewer than twelve footmen, a bimonthly mass flagellation, and taking her meals from the naked posteriors of a young serving girl, piping hot omelette being a personal favourite. In the circumstances one might expect her to encounter difficulties in recruiting staff, but this is not the case. Competition for posts is keen, as it is for her favours. *See fig. 37*

{Fig. 37} 'Piping hot omelette being a personal favourite'

Sapphism

Carnal indulgence between women, a subject of which I have made a particular study. The practice is considered by some to be an impossibility, by others an absurdity, by still others as occurring only under the influence of debased men for their own private satisfaction. Of these three hypotheses, all are demonstrably untrue, the first two being the product of naivety and an understandable desire to find innocence in the fair sex, the third, known as the pseudosapphic theorem, a misconception brought about by a lack of proper investigation.

Readers must forgive me a small excursion here, in examining the work of Dr T----- S------, who has, in recent years, been the principal proponent of the pseudosapphic theorem. Firstly, I feel it my duty to point out that in order to obtain the various degrees of which he makes so much, the Doctor read law, philosophy and the classics, worthy enough subjects no doubt, but unsuited to the rigorous application of scientific principles. Therefore his poor methodology will come as no surprise when we learn that he conducted his studies exclusively in houses of ill repute, and Parisian ones at that, where he drew his conclusions from the high proportion of ladies of negotiable virtue who would perform sapphic acts but only when paid to do so. No great intelligence is required to see the falsity of this reasoning, and I shall therefore detain the reader no longer.

My own, properly conducted, researches demonstrate beyond doubt that sapphism is a very real vice, and by no means uncommon. In order to make my observations without fear of prejudicing the subjects it has been necessary to remain unobserved, allowing the participants unrestrained indulgence of their beastly habits, and in order to be absolutely certain that their motive is the indulgence of each other in carnal pleasure, to remain *in situ* until a condition of erotic hysteria has been reached.

I have cited numerous examples of sapphic congress elsewhere in this work, which it would be superfluous to repeat. One example will suffice as irrefutable proof of my position: those observations made, and sketched, in the course of a single night spent perched in a large cypress tree opposite the dormitory block of S---- M-----'s Convent School, near P---------, Berkshire. Thus situated, and equipped with an excellent pair of binoculars, I observed no fewer than twelve instances of sapphic indulgence: five between pairs of girls, four between nuns and girls, two involving three girls together, and one involving five nuns and a single girl of truly rapacious masochistic appetite, during the climax of which I had the misfortune to fall from the tree on to a set of cucumber frames, the noise of which obliged me to make a retreat for fear of ruining the scientific purity of my observations.

Seduction

The wretched practice of seeking carnal gratification while avoiding the attendant responsibilities, a beastly act in itself and all too often one that leads to other forms of beastliness.

The fundamental aim of the seducer is to gain his carnal satisfaction, on which he places an inordinate value, considering the mere pampering of his glands more important than a lady's virtue, honour or position, and indeed, more important than his own virtue or honour and position, to say nothing of his personal safety. Inevitably such fellows are immoral in other ways as well, and it is rare for the seducer to be content with the simpler and less sinful expressions of carnality. Furthermore, although he knows neither guilt nor remorse, he must walk abroad in constant fear of retaliation, for John Bull is not one to meekly accept the mistreatment of his wives and sisters, nor his daughters and nieces, and, as the old saying goes, one may as well be hung for a sheep as for a lamb. Thus, any fair flower who falls into the clutches of a seducer is likely to be taken full advantage of, subjected to all manner of fornication and left not only bereft of her virtue but irredeemably corrupted.

Such was the fate of Miss E---- T----, whom I first knew as a girl so shy that even to look into the eyes of a man seemed to cause her physical pain, but who, after studying in Paris for a number of years and being seduced by an artist, returned to England as a bold and salacious creature who once suggested that a garden party at the Rectory would be enlivened if she removed her clothes for the edification of my guests.

In the case of Miss T----, the artist, one Monsieur A----- J----, had apparently overcome both her natural defences and those taught her by the nuns of St Mary's Convent, Upminster, through a combination of the judicious administration of absinthe, long expositions on the expression of freedom through nudity, and unstinting flattery. These are just three of the many weapons to be found in the seducer's arsenal, although he did not use the commonest of all, which is false promise.

So prevalent is this technique, and so widely reported, that I am astonished it seems to be so effective. Essentially, the seducer pays court to his quarry for a while, plights his troth and then declares his love so ardent that he is unable to wait for consummation on their wedding night. Thinking they are to be married anyway, and deeply in love with the scheming swine, the lady surrenders herself, only to be abandoned once he has taken his fill of her charms. This happens at least a hundred times each year in England alone, leading me to despair of the gullibility of the fairer sex almost as much as the depravity of the less fair.

In addition to false promise, intoxication, persuasion and flattery, a moderately common and quite successful technique is for the seducer to appeal to a lady's sense of obligation, such as contriving to make the settlement of a debt at cards subject to the removal of her clothes or even a lewd act. Base threats and blackmail may also be used, as well as bribery, although in this last case one might very well argue that if a lady is prepared to accept payment for the surrender of her virtue then it is already too late.

The great majority of seducers at least have the decency to keep their deplorable behaviour to themselves, if only because to boast abroad must inevitably hamper their chances of making new conquests. However, among those of high wealth but low morals, seduction can become something of a sport, and I have even known wagers to be placed on whether a particular lady will succumb to blandishment, which subject provides both an excellent illustration of this beastly vice and a caution against the sin of hubris.

Lord K-------- was probably the most single-mindedly debauched rake of his era, following an outrageous career from his arrival in society in 1779 to his death in 1794, which included thirty-six known seductions, of which he would boast without the slightest regard for propriety, modesty or consequence. He was known to be a superb shot and a devil with a rapier, winning nine duels across the years, although it was his preferred practice to pay the families of his victims off, and with a gesture of utter contempt, throwing the money on the ground for them to pick up.

It was the boast of this odious fellow that he could seduce any woman, old or young, high-born or low. One drunken evening his almost equally odious friend, Sir J----- V---, offered a wager that Lord K-------- would fail to succeed in the case of a young Scottish girl of his acquaintance, Miss J--- M-------. The wager was duly accepted and the girl seduced, but not easily. At first she would submit only to the use of her hand, which Sir J----- declared inadequate, then to irrumation, which Sir J----- again declared inadequate. Finally, after some months and nightly encounters involving all sorts of depravity, Lord K-------- persuaded Miss M------- to lift her skirts and allow him access, only to discover that his supposed conquest was in fact a man.

Unsurprisingly, this made Lord K-------- a laughing stock among his set, and so great was his rage that he challenged Sir J----- to a duel, intending to kill him, but on their arrival at Tuthill Fields they were accosted by 'Miss' M-------, whose opinion on the matter they had failed to take into account, and who shot them both.

Sodomy

That sin for which God destroyed the city of Sodom. This is generally assumed to mean lavenderistic proctism, and by the law and the learned to imply that the inhabitants of that city were in the habit of inserting their virile members in any convenient receptacle without reference to morality or procreative need. However, the Bible makes no such clear statement.

The passages in question reveal only that the Sodomites seemed to consider the arrival of two male strangers in the city as an excellent excuse for some form of orgy. Lot's offer of his daughters was rejected, which is generally taken as evidence of lavenderism on the part of the Sodomites, but we know that Sodom was a thriving city at the time, so the inhabitants may have been erotoaplistiacs, but they were not purely lavenderistic or the city would have speedily gone into decline. This apparent contradiction may be explained if we assume that it was the custom among the Sodomites to greet all strangers in this fashion, demanding the satisfaction of their lusts by any means convenient, hence the legal and learned definition of sodomy, while it is no surprise at all that their behaviour incited the wrath of God.

Spanking

Britain's principal form of beastliness, save only onanism, in that it is more widely practised than any other, among both men and women, and with roughly equal preference for giving or receiving. Why so many have come to corrupt such a simple and essentially harmless form of domestic discipline into a carnal activity is not immediately apparent, although I have formed distinct theories on the subject, which I examine below.

{Fig. 38} 'Why so many have come to corrupt such a simple and essentially harmless form of domestic discipline into a carnal activity is not immediately apparent'

First we must consider the dynamics of this beastly practice. Spanking, as strictly defined, involves the brisk and forceful application of the hand to the posteriors, but even within this apparently simple formula there is extraordinary variation. In studying these factors let us, for the sake of simplicity, consider them from the perspective of a gentleman spanking a lady.

Position: I have catalogued over two dozen distinct positions which the receiver may be made to adopt, including standing, kneeling, lying over the knee, on her back with her legs raised, touching her toes and even standing on her hands. Most are designed to bring the posteriors into prominence, and also to fill the lady in question with very understandable embarrassment, which appears to exist no matter how great her pleasure in the treatment. Of these positions, lying across the knee is much the most popular, among all groups and in particular in the case of sapphic spanking, for which I found it to be employed in seventy-seven cases out of the hundred.

Clothing: so common is the practice of baring the posteriors in order for a spanking to be administered that it must be considered standard. Indeed, many practitioners are obsessive about this detail, those on the receiving end no less than those who are giving. The posteriors, it seems, must be bare. How this is done is less simple, with many an elaborate ritual designed to maximise the sense of exposure and shame for the lady who is about to be spanked, to such an extent that simply lifting her skirts and opening her drawers must be considered exceptional, even crass. In rare cases, generally when those involved are still, as it were, testing the water, or the spanking is being given in a public place, a lady may be allowed to retain that limited modesty afforded by the seat of her drawers, or even her petticoats. Only during the most simple or preliminary exchanges is a lady ever permitted to retain the covering of her dress.

Technique: it would be simplistic to suppose that merely applying the flat of the hand to the fullest part of a lady's posteriors is sufficient to satisfy the elaborate cravings of the carnally inclined. Far from it: many techniques exist. Examples include using only the tips of the fingers and a curious flapping motion of the hand to produce a sharp, stinging sensation; cupping the hand in order to make a loud, clapping sound, which is especially embarrassing as it draws attention to the lady's plight; and, lewdest of all, applying the hand to the turn of the posteriors so that each smack sends a sharp jolt to the lady's most intimate parts, not infrequently inducing a state of erotic hysteria.

Scolding: forms a common, even usual, adjunct to spanking, the purpose being for the gentleman to bring home to the lady across his knee the full effect of what is being done to her. Ironically, given his own outrageous conduct, this frequently includes chiding her for immorality, indecency or a lack of maidenly modesty, but he may also remark on some real or imagined sin or misconduct and, in order to heighten her embarrassment and his own enjoyment, make the most intimate and improper observations on the dishevelled state of her dress or even those charms the display of which she is so helpless to prevent.

Aftermath: one might imagine that after such a beastly performance those involved might be so inflamed that they would immediately give themselves over to their basest passions without restraint, and indeed this is often the case. However, in practice the ritual often continues in one of two forms, either with the lady being sent to stand in one corner of the room with her hands on her head and her posteriors bare, that she may spend a while in contemplation of her misdeeds and their consequences, or by the gentleman applying a soothing lotion to her heated skin. Only then is passion given free rein.

So our hypothetical lady has been spanked, but why did the gentleman feel it necessary to do this to her, and why did she desire it to be done? I have been able to elucidate three possibilities, which may well exist in tandem.

One: by diligent research I have discovered that in both men and women the heating of the posteriors, such as is achieved by a vigorous spanking, draws blood to the intimate areas of the body, resulting in arousal and even emission or erotic hysteria, depending on the sex, without further stimulation. In certain positions there is also the matter of friction between the private parts of the spanked and the leg of the spanker.

Two: relating to the above but of a cerebral rather than physical nature, I postulate that those who suffer from extreme erotic incontinence may grow excited by both the exposure of their posteriors and the touch of a hand to their naked flesh, rather than suffer the pain and shame one would typically, and properly, associate with receiving a bare-bottom spanking.

Three: some, those of notably insubordinate character, may turn this form of chastisement to pleasure in deliberate defiance of propriety and mockery of all that is godly. This may seem improbable, but in support of my theory I cite the case of Miss V----- F-------, who was spanked daily in a full and elaborate ritual in an attempt to cure her of onanism. This took place over a period of seven years, the spanking being delivered on her bare posteriors and with an audience consisting of myself as the local vicar, two curates, selected neighbours, the servants and on one occasion a visiting bishop; but it failed to cure her of the habit. One might suspect mere obstinacy, were it not for the observed fact that she only ever indulged her lewd habit at five o'clock in the afternoon and with the door of her room wide open, so that those assembled for afternoon tea could hardly fail to notice, and to react in the manner she evidently desired. *See fig. 38*

Spectophilia

More commonly referred to as voyeurism, this is the habit of watching others for purposes of carnal arousal, generally while those others are in a state of partial or complete undress. No doubt this depraved and despicable practice is almost as old as clothes themselves, and it is quite easy to imagine some early, cave-dwelling man watching his female counterpart at work tending the fire in the hope that, should she bend over sufficiently, her uncured elk-hide skirt will rise far enough to afford him a glimpse of a pair of well-turned posteriors.

{Fig. 39} 'The voyeur is frequently to be found at seaside resorts'

No such simple gratification is available to modern man, save only in the very strongest of gales, during which no lady who wishes to preserve her modesty should go out, owing to the propensity of powerful gusts of wind to lift skirts, petticoats and all, thus leaving her drawers or possibly even more on display to all and sundry. No, the extensive and modest clothing worn by respectable women of today has forced the voyeur to become a creature of skulking cunning, devising ever more elaborate means to steal a glimpse of the forbidden, and as his artifice and determination grows, so must the efforts of the lady who is his natural prey, in order that she may protect herself.

Thus we find our womenfolk bedecked in petticoats that conceal all but the occasional glimpse of boot, and subsidiary petticoats that conceal the lace of the first petticoat, lest even that should give the potential voyeur cause for satisfaction. Collars are worn high to the neck, gloves conceal the hands, and veils are by no means uncommon, all this in order that the daughters of Eve may protect their fair forms from the vulgar and voyeuristic gaze.

In response to this, the voyeur has been forced to extreme measures, and some have even devoted much of their lives and not inconsiderable fortunes to the pursuit of that elusive glimpse of unguarded female flesh. Yet even the most ardent of voyeurs remains keen to avoid the attentions of Her Majesty's Constabulary, and so those prepared to peer in at windows or conceal themselves in cupboards, to drill carefully concealed holes in the walls of rooms, or to construct elaborate systems of mirrors to obtain views at improbable angles, are rare. More common are those who wish to be able to present an excuse for their conduct in the event of being caught.

Thus the voyeur is frequently to be found at seaside resorts, where the necessity of undressing in order to bathe appears to be an irresistible lure, yet even here he has no easy task. The introduction of bathing machines must have come as a baffling development, and forced him to frequent ever more obscure resorts as they spread, until I suspect that the majority have been forced abroad, to slake their appetites upon the women of less modest nations, particularly in the tropics. It is my personal theory that this exodus has played a small but not unimportant part in the growth of Empire. *See fig. 39*

Strap

An implement favoured among the lower orders for purposes of carnal flagellation, the strap is a simple length of leather, sometimes not even shaped, but effective enough for those who care nothing for elegance or style. The belt may also be included here and is notable only that it is most frequently employed by an even lower order of fellows, and yet, in one of those curious reversals so typical of the entire subject of depravity, it is notably popular among the better class of female masochist, as well as those who like to wield it for purposes of erotic flagellation.

Thus we have Lady C------- B------ B--------, the daughter of a Royal Duke and of unimpeachable pedigree, who makes frequent visits to those poorer cottages of her neighbourhood occupied by unmarried men. She will bring bread and cheese, or perhaps a nutritious soup, but before giving of her charity she will demand of the man that he take his belt to her posteriors, ostensibly as a means of displaying her humility, but given what tends to happen afterwards I cannot say that I am entirely convinced by this argument.

Subligariophilia

The association of carnality with undergarments. As with all paraphilias, variety exists, and no doubt case studies may be made of a wide range of individuals who have developed unhealthy obsessions with a wide range of undergarments, but my own researches show that in more than nine cases out of every ten this fetish takes the form of male fascination with female drawers, stockings or corsets, sometimes all three simultaneously. Corsets and stockings are dealt with separately, while the chemise and combination underwear are generally looked down upon by the true enthusiast, who concentrates on drawers.

Given the existence of such an obsession, one might hope that a subligariophiliac might be content with observing his wife in a pair of pretty drawers. Is it, perhaps, not wholly ungodly to admit that these subtle confections of silk or cotton, lace and embroidery make a pleasant enhancement to the female form, while the panel-backed and split-seam varieties allow possibilities of yet more intimate glimpses, which must surely delight those of a carnal nature? Sadly, no. All such things are enjoyed by the subligariophiliac, on his wife, on other ladies as available and in pictorial or photographic form, but I regret to report that many, perhaps even the majority, hold this as insufficient. Indeed, in many cases their beastly lust would seem to be unquenchable.

More than any other paraphiliac, the subligariophiliac is a hoarder, often amassing huge collections of female underwear. Nor does he tend to be content with purchasing such items from suitably appointed emporia, but prefers to steal those already worn, not for reasons of thrift or the bashfulness natural to a male entering an establishment catering for ladies, but out of sheer licentiousness, for to the subligariophiliac the great virtue of an item of intimate apparel is that it has been in contact with the body of the lady in question. Low fellows indeed, and some lower than others, for while the generally accepted technique of acquisition is to prowl laundries and lurk beside washing lines in the hope of making a sudden snatch at a suitable garment, there are those who only consider a pair of drawers truly won if they are removed from the lady while she is wearing them, and not necessarily with her agreement.

The most notorious exponent of this bizarre and deplorable habit must surely have been the eighth Baron G----, who, on his death, was discovered to possess a collection of no fewer than three thousand four hundred and sixteen pairs of ladies' drawers, each and every one carefully labelled with the date and manner of acquisition, including seductions, purchases from ladies, purchases from husbands and lovers, thefts from washing lines and laundries, and, in pride of place, what we may term outrage thefts, when his accomplice, the butler and a confirmed tetigilagniac, would tickle the unfortunate lady beneath her arms, thus rendering her unable to defend herself against the removal of her drawers from beneath her skirts.

Another characteristic of this depravity, and the Baron's particular pleasure, is a preference for high-quality drawers. Not for Baron G---- a simple pair of split-seam linen drawers as might be found on a plain and honest washerwoman, nor indeed the extraordinary confections of frills and lace favoured by the harlot and the *demi-mondaine*, although his collection contained plenty of both sorts and every variety between; but rather, and in pride of place in glass-fronted display cabinets set along the upper passages of his house, fine, voluminous garments of heavy silk, lace-trimmed, decorated with tasteful embroidery and closing at the back by means of a panel fastened up by as many as a dozen buttons. Such are the drawers originally worn by Lady C-------- F-------, younger daughter of the Earl of B-------, removed by outrageous theft on the evening of the twenty-third of April, 1893, and subsequently placed on display by the Baron along with a detailed record of how he and his fiendish accomplice spent some half an hour watching her bathe, but waited until she had pulled her drawers up before accosting her and stealing the garment, an act of despicable depravity and yet also a classic illustration of paraphiliac behaviour.

It is possible that yet more illuminating outrages wait to be revealed, but the Baron's collection is a large one and I have not yet finished cataloguing it and adapting his system of classification to my own.

Submission

The surrender of one's will to that of another for purposes of carnal gratification. This is a common feature of depraved practice, and although one might consider the submission of a wife to her husband's need an act of charity or even virtue, I have found that this is seldom the case. More frequently she makes this gesture in order to facilitate the satisfaction of some strange and sinister fascination, or, if not, in order to provide herself an excuse for giving in to her very basest needs. The same applies to the male.

Indeed, in my considered opinion, 'submission' is something of a misnomer, as with very few exceptions it is the partner who has in theory surrendered who chooses both the nature and extent of whatever beastly indulgences occur. A case in point is that of Dr T------ C-----, whose personal vice was to dress as a maid and serve tea to his wife and certain female accomplices. To this end he would don a full and elaborate uniform, including stockings, combinations and corset of plain white linen, a black bombazine dress, gloves, heeled boots and a small hat set on top of a wig of remarkable volume. He would then perform all those tasks normally appropriate for a house maid, but most specifically the service of tea, at which his wife and her friends were obliged to wear fine, stiff-necked gowns of pure black taffeta, all made to the order of the doctor himself, and knee-length boots of supple black leather equipped with an elaborate system of double lacing. With six ladies thus attired, one must doubt his claim to have been their obedient and humble servant, and rather see him as he was, a manipulative old goat with a penchant for transvestism and the facade, if not the substance, of female domination.

In the course of my researches I have come across very few cases of genuine submission, which is to say, that in which one partner genuinely wishes to give themself over to the whims of the other without stint. Even then, the recipient of such favours is often found wanting, forcing the submissive to move on to fresh pastures. A typical example is provided by Miss L--- F------, a young lady of charm, good education and personable disposition whose greatest desire was to be used as a toy for the carnal gratification of men. Her first husband declined to share her with others and was speedily abandoned. Her second husband shared her too often and was also abandoned. Her third husband declined to give her over to the cruelties of other women and he too was abandoned. Her fourth and fifth husbands died of carnal apoplexy. Her sixth became a lunatic in his efforts to satisfy her desires and her seventh survives only because by then I had decided that enough was enough and so, in an act of Christian charity, accepted her as a maid in my own establishment.

Sus Eroticus

An example of animal transformation fantasy in which the subject takes on the characteristics of the domestic pig (*Sus scrofa*).

In its simple, rustic form this differs little from mudlarking, and often involves no more than a man standing over his paramour, perhaps armed with a switch cut from the hedgerow, while she, naked, wallows in mud, snuffles up acorns with her lips and generally indulges in pig-like behaviour. As with the hogtie, this practice is commonest in those parts of the country traditionally associated with pig farming, and I have observed more examples in Wiltshire than in any other three counties combined. In such circumstances the term 'piggy-girl' is generally employed.

In more elaborate versions of this depraved game the girl, or man, may be fitted with a pink rubber snout and a curled tail, both items attached to the body with the aid of stage glue, thus greatly enhancing the piggy nature of the subject. In Gloucestershire, where the Old Spot pig is the predominant breed, Mr S----- G---- of Much Ash Farm goes further still, employing not only tail and snout but black stage paint to ensure than when he takes his wife out to the wallow she resembles as fully as possible the local variety.

Still more ingenious is Monsieur C----- A------- of Toulouse, France, who is in the habit of taking his wife, her sister and their niece out together to the local woods. Here the girls strip naked, apply snouts and tails in the traditional manner and don leather truffle harnesses, fashioned to precisely the same function as those used for real pigs, so that while the three girls are able to rootle freely among the leaves and earth of the forest floor, they are unable to consume any delicacies they should happen upon. That this practice is an outrage to both decency and dignity there can

{Fig. 40} 'In its simple, rustic form this differs little from mudlarking'

be no doubt, and yet if M. A------- is to be believed he has managed to train his girls
in the searching out of truffles to such good effect that they are able to compete in
the annual truffle hunt, in which on one occasion his sister-in-law was placed third.
See fig. 40

Switches

Crude devices of chastisement and therefore inevitably also of erotic
chastisement, formed of the raw plucked shoots of one or another species
of plant, including, but not limited to, willow, ash, apple, holly, broom, reeds and
certain sedges, but most notably birch, which is dealt with in detail above.

The switch is a rustic device, as one might expect, and most generally found
in use as a substitute for the cane in poorer households or among those who have
not had the benefit of a proper education. One highly regrettable exception exists,
related to the peculiar taste found occasionally among ladies of the highest birth for
men of the very lowest, when the lady in question also happens to be of masochistic
temperament. Lady C------- B------ B--------, the devotee of the strap, also makes a
habit of donning servants' clothing and visiting the local quarry. Here she will select
one of the most robust among the quarrymen and taunt him in the most outrageous
manner while flourishing a crude switch of her own selection. Her remarks vary,
but their essence is always a challenge to the quarryman to prove his manhood
by applying the switch to her posteriors, which she will often flaunt in order to
further encourage him. Simple men that they are, few quarrymen can resist such
blandishments, and still less the immodest arts she applies to their members once
she has been warmed behind.

Switching

Primarily, the application of a switch, as described, to the posteriors of another for purposes of carnal stimulation. Secondarily, the habit of indulgence in nominally opposite vices, such as sadism and masochism, or domination and submission, by a single person, either consecutively or, more rarely, concurrently.

Certain authorities regard the second as an impossibility, but this is merely a consequence of interviewing those of a debauched but inflexible nature rather than drawing their conclusions from pure observation. My erstwhile colleague Sir C----- V---, for instance, states in his treatise on aberrant desires that sadism and masochism are mutually exclusive paraphilias, but with due respect Sir C----- would do better to spend less time in the rarefied atmosphere of the college hospital and more time out in the field, as I do.

Not only is it possible for one individual to enjoy two apparently contradictory paraphilias, but I have recorded several instances of deviants doing precisely that and at the same time. At his country estate Lord C------ used to spank his wife while simultaneously being flagellated and criticised for his technique by a trio of ladies of negotiable virtue from nearby Guildford. Mr R--- M------- of Aberdeen used to allow himself to be dressed in a dog suit and exercised on the local heath by his wife, but they would also dress their maid in similar fashion so that he might chase and mount her, while each successful copulation would in turn result in a severe switching for both master and maid. Mrs E---- S------- liked to seat herself on her husband's head while she in turned was suckled from the teat of her Jamaican nurse, and so it goes on, case after case, each one proving my position beyond all compromise or doubt.

Tattoos

The relationship between the tattoo and carnal desire is a curious one and by no means simple. Indeed, I have identified four entirely distinct penchants relating to tattoos and the process of tattooing, which may exist separately or in combination.

Most frequent is the use of tattoos as a form of display, a largely male phenomenon which has a curious parallel in the world of birds. Thus, as a peacock (*Pavo cristatus*) struts his glorious tail, or the ruff cock (*Philomachus pugnax*) spreads his neck feathers, so the sailor wears a tattooed anchor on his manly upper arm, or the roustabout an image of a scantily clad girl of voluptuous proportions. In every case the aim is to attract the female of the species, lavenderists excepted, and although I am unable to furnish exact data, it would seem to be effective.

In reflection of the above is that curious and beastly fascination occasionally observed among women of high status with their social inferiors, in which tattoos often play a part. The Duchess of D-----, for instance, is known to be in the habit of dressing as a menial in order that she may visit the dockside areas of Weymouth and Poole, where she will urge sailors to compete in the display of their tattoos, with the promise of carnal indulgence for the winner. A fair-minded but somewhat indecisive young woman, she frequently finds herself unable to declare a single winner and thus is sometimes obliged to submit herself to six or even ten of the competitors simultaneously.

More beastly still is the ponolagniac practice of achieving carnal arousal through the pain of tattooing. This is rare, and carries the disadvantage that while the desire is addictive, the surface area of the human body is limited, with consequences as inevitable as they are regrettable. The sad outcome of this peculiar lust may be observed at circuses up and down the land, although the starkest warning against the practice is provided by the case of Mr G----- P-----,

{Fig. 41} 'That curious and beastly fascination occasionally observed
among women of high status with their social inferiors'

who on his demise was discovered to be blue in colour from the top of his bald head to the tips of his toes.

Lastly, and perhaps somewhat tangential, is the secretive and sinister practice of tattooing for the purposes of carnal symbolism. Thus, by sporting tiny but distinctive tattoos, men or women may betray themselves as available for the satiation of excess lust, or as adherents to specific beastly practices, all unbeknownst to the respectable people around them. I have made something of a study of this and intend to publish a small monograph, but for the time being I will reveal that a Cupid's bow indicates a penchant for irrumation, a high-heeled boot a desire to worship such an article, and a horseshoe a need for Equus Eroticus. *See fig. 41*

Tawse

An implement of chastisement favoured by the inhabitants of Scotland and all too frequently misused for beastly purposes rather than domestic or scholastic discipline.

A typical tawse is twelve to eighteen inches in length and anything from one to four inches in width, with a shaped handle, a midsection and a sting cut longitudinally into two, three or more rarely four tails. A good tawse will be between one quarter and one half of an inch thick, and made from well-cured back leather taken from the hide of an elderly bull. In certain remote parts of Scotland it is the habit of farmers to leave their bulls to reach as grand an age as possible, thus ensuring a ready supply of the best-quality tawse leather.

Traditionally, tawses may be divided into the lighter, two-tailed variety characteristic of the lowlands and urban areas, and the heavier, three-tailed variety found in the highlands and islands, where the sturdier, more resilient posteriors of the inhabitants demand firmer treatment. This I have found to be a myth, although the rare four-tailed tawse does appear to be almost entirely confined to the island of

Benbecula. More recently, with the rise of industrial manufacture, firms have sprung up that produce a full range of implements of every weight and style. The best known of these is J--- J D--- of Lochgelly.

Leaving aside the correct application of the tawse, let us consider its improper use, as exemplified by carnal flagellants not only in Scotland itself but in every corner of the globe to which that hardy race has spread. Initially, a typical flagellant's ritual is followed, in mockery of ordinary discipline, with the woman's skirts raised and her drawers pulled wide to expose her posteriors before she adopts a suitable pose, generally with her upper body resting on some suitable piece of furniture with her hips thrust upwards and outwards to provide her husband, or other partner, with the best possible target. The tawse is then applied, the wielder using a characteristic swinging motion designed to bring the full width of the implement down evenly across the posteriors of the unfortunate recipient, who is seldom able to contain her cries, but will nevertheless be rapidly reduced to a condition of helpless arousal of which the man may be expected to take full advantage.

Tetigilagnia

A most pernicious form of beastliness, used by the debased male in order to take advantage of feminine susceptibility by tickling, and by the debased female in order to find an excuse for the expression of hysterical inclination. On rare occasions the situation may be reversed, but for practical purposes erotic tickling may be considered from two angles, that of the male tickler and that of the female who desires to be tickled.

The tickler is a low fellow, a cad and a bounder, although I am sorry to say as common among the upper echelons of society as elsewhere. By stealthy behaviour and the pretence of harmless, albeit intrusively intimate, playfulness, he will inflict his penchant on any convenient female he happens to desire. Thus he hopes to

{Fig. 42} 'At last, when thoroughly tickled, she will be able to attain, or feign, a
condition of such absolute physical helplessness that she is unable to rise'

enjoy her helpless response and at the same time intimate bodily contact, be it a light giggle and the brush of his fingers against the curve of breast or hip, or, if brought to a successful conclusion, helpless wriggling as she descends into a state of collapse, this accompanied by the display of her most intimate parts, into which he may then plunge his by then engorged member without fear of resistance.

His natural counterpart is the female hysteric who finds being tickled a pleasurable or convenient route for the expression of her carnality. First, she will encourage the gentleman of her choice to tickle her. If she is successful in this endeavour, she will then giggle, squirm, adopt erotic poses and even press herself against him until in inevitable consequence of her behaviour he grows aroused. At last, when thoroughly tickled, she will be able to attain, or feign, a condition of such absolute physical helplessness that she is unable to rise from the floor, upon which she can with a little artifice ensure that her skirts fall open and her thighs come apart, thus displaying herself in quite as lewd a manner as can possibly be imagined, but with minimal risk of moral censure, for if called to task she need merely protest that the tickling robbed her of all ability to control herself. Thus spread, and excited by the indulgence of her beastly penchant, she will be mounted, for what man could resist such a sight as she will be presenting?

Tetigilagnia is notably common among the theatrical profession and those who patronise theatres and music halls, possibly due to the ready availability of ostrich feathers in such establishments. The moral values of such people are also not what they might be, and it is not uncommon to observe quite open tickling and other mild depravities when behind the scenes, even at the opera. *See fig. 42*

Theaphilia

A practice not only beastly but verging on the sacrilegious in that it involves the worship of a woman as if she were a goddess.

This is, to the limit of my research, an exclusively male preoccupation, possibly because women have too much common sense. The number of women who wish to be treated in this manner is also low, largely, so I understand, because it requires a great deal of effort to live up to the expectations of the typical theaphile. Thus we have the first irony of the situation, in that while the theaphile wishes to worship at the feet of his 'goddess', he is almost without exception the most demanding of creatures. A typical example is provided by Mr B------- K--- of Bloomsbury, who lives in the cellar of his townhouse, naked at all times, is fed on kitchen scraps, and crawls to the top of his stairs once a day to lick the soles of his paramour's boots and gaze up at her in adoration before crawling back to his bare mattress for the brief moment of frenzied onanism that is his sole satisfaction. The position of his paramour, Miss J---- G----, might seem enviable, until one considers that she must keep herself immaculate at all times and in a constant state of readiness to provide for him, while, as he deems himself unworthy to touch her in any way, she must take her own pleasure in secret, with the chimney sweep or the baker's boy as circumstances dictate.

Inevitably, ladies of negotiable virtue have been quick to take advantage of such weakness, and we therefore have the second irony of these 'goddesses' usually being women of the lowest moral character. Many houses of ill repute have a 'goddess' in regular employment, generally a tall woman of stern appearance who is notably skilled in the arts of bondage and flagellation, and those that do not are generally able to supply a girl to perform the function at quite short notice. In some cases, theaphilia has even proved the route to wealth, mainly when the adulation takes a distinctive form, with the man wishing to make himself utterly dependent on the object of his desire. Thus we have the example of the American industrialist Mr P--- J Z------------, who signed over his entire fortune to a Miss M----- R------ of Richmond, Virginia, on the promise of being made her houseboy. To do Miss R------ due credit, rather than abscond with his wealth she appears to have complied with his wishes, and was frequently to be seen reclining in a hammock over a leisurely glass of mint julep while he cut the lawn with a pair of Messrs H----- & D-------'s patent corn scissors.

Theatre

A most disreputable form of entertainment, long associated with harlots, strumpets, fortune hunters and those of generally low moral character, both male and female, along with the rakes, roués, queans and frivolous women they attract. Why this should be is not immediately clear, for there is nothing inherently immoral in the practice of acting. Indeed, I myself have arranged the occasional parish entertainment to no ill effect. However, a visit to any stage door in the land at the right hour will prove the truth of my assertion, as there you will witness every form of improper assignation, from unattended beauties climbing into gentlemen's carriages to, in extreme cases, lewd acts performed in convenient alleyways. As if such behaviour were not bad enough, in recent years the public have taken to lauding both actors and actresses, such as Miss L--- M----- and Mrs L--- L------, as if they had performed some great public service rather than merely postured upon a stage, while their indiscretions are ignored or even admired.

Warning is frequently given to young women to avoid the stage for fear of encountering those who would seek to corrupt them, which is good advice, but I have found that the reverse is equally true, and that young men attending the theatre should beware of the temptations likely to be placed before them. Indeed, my advice would be that no person should attend any such establishment until they have attained an age at which they may make mature and seasoned judgements. Only thus may they avoid the snares laid for them by unprincipled young women seeking advantage and, worse, lavenderists.

I myself have suffered such attentions when, as a young curate, I regularly attended the theatre so that I might witness for myself those depravities associated with the profession. Following one performance I chanced to fall into conversation with what seemed a most respectable gentleman, although at the time I recall thinking that his scent was unnecessarily strong and his choice of dress perhaps a trifle extravagant. Nonetheless, he seemed a pleasant enough fellow, and it was a cold night with a long walk back to my lodgings in prospect, so I gratefully accepted his offer of a glass of hot claret cup at his house in Bloomsbury. You may imagine my horror when, after no more than perhaps five or six glasses, he attempted an unspeakable intimacy upon my person, and it was only my youth, vigour and the fortunate proximity of a stuffed badger (*Meles meles*) with which to fend off his advances that enabled me to make my escape.

Thyrsoadoria

Describes the worship of the virile member. By worship I do not refer to that simple enjoyment which even a virtuous woman might acknowledge, if only in the privacy of her own thoughts, but to a full-blown veneration in which all sense of modesty or reserve is abandoned.

Curious though it may seem, thyrsoadoria is not especially common even among the lewdest of women, who tend to appreciate the virile member for the pleasure it can bring them rather than for its own sake. The true thyrsoadoriac, by contrast, makes the virile member the focus of her entire being, to the exclusion of all else, including the man to whom the object of her desire is affixed. Thus, so far as men are concerned, thyrsoadoria is not as desirable in the female as might be supposed.

Mrs C------- S----- of Honeysuckle Cottage, Trenthide-on-the-Wold, Gloucestershire, provides a case in point. Each evening, she demands that her husband sit in an armchair by the fire. Placing a sheepskin rug on the floor, she will kneel at his feet, where she will perform a lengthy and elaborate act of irrumation while simultaneously indulging her own base needs by hand. This may sound all very jolly for Mr S-----, who is not above depravity himself, but woe betide him if he attempts to vary the routine or, worse, achieves his own satisfaction before she is entirely finished. Her tongue is sharp and her aim excellent.

This is also a common depravity among men, both lavenderists, among whom it might even be said to be universal, and narcissists. In both cases I have noted an obsession with size, often taken to such lengths as to become comical. This is well illustrated by the lewd drawings of Mr A----- B--------, in some of which the virile member is portrayed as so grotesquely out of proportion to the rest of the body that any person so endowed in reality would immediately fall flat on his face.

Transvestism

The practice of dressing in clothing normally associated with the opposite sex. This takes many forms, and differs from androgyny in that the intention is not necessarily to mimic the opposite sex but merely to assume the clothing thereof. The notorious Rector of W-----------, for example, enjoyed parading in his garden dressed in the underwear of his housekeeper, but, at over twenty stone in weight and heavily bearded, it is unreasonable to suppose that he intended to appear as a woman.

In considering transvestism as a form of beastliness we need not dwell upon the merely vulgar, such as men dressing as women in order to take part in music-hall acts, nor do we need to consider theatrical transvestism, although in the latter case I have my doubts.

According to popular myth transvestism is closely associated with lavenderism, and indeed one might be forgiven for thinking this logical, but it is not the case. Nor is it an exclusively male habit, although female transvestites are undoubtedly in the minority. In practice, so varied are the motives for carnal transvestism that it becomes impossible to list typical characteristics. In some cases it is a solitary activity, indulged purely for the physical sensation. For others it may allow them to enjoy experiences and characteristics more usually associated with the opposite sex, such as the innate vulnerability or the right to play the coquette enjoyed by females but not males, or, in reverse, the authority and forceful behaviour expected of the male. Still others take pleasure in the very shame of their own beastliness and often require chastisement while in their unnatural clothes, generally from a stern and beautiful member of the sex whose apparel they have taken on.

If there is a consistent factor to transvestism, then it must be the preference for grand or flamboyant clothing. Rare indeed is the male transvestite who is content with a plain frock, or his female counterpart who willingly dons the rough clothes of the tradesman or factory worker. Exaggeration is rather the rule, in some case to the point of pastiche, with the man lost in a gigantic array of frills and lace, feathers and frippery of all sorts, while the female is most likely to be in a smart military uniform, perhaps that of the Guards, with her scarlet tunic worn tight over nubile breasts and her trousers fitting like a second skin to the rounded contours of her thighs, belly and posterior charms.

Tribolagnia

Commonly known as frottage, this is a disgraceful practice whereby the offender, or 'frotteur', will rub parts of his, or more rarely her, body against the unsuspecting object of their admiration. This is a low and surreptitious habit most commonly found among those who travel in crowded trains, patronise the cheaper enclosures at race meetings and attend gala events such as jubilees, or it may be that such events simply attract frotteurs.

Either way, my researches indicate that the typical frotteur is a man of middle age, middle class and middling appearance: in short, exactly the sort of person an attractive young lady would be least likely to notice, a fact that enables him to draw close and indulge his beastly habit. So cunning are these individuals that they have adopted a favourite practice of entering the most crowded carriages on the subterranean sections of the Metropolitan and District Railways, where the close proximity of the passengers and the rhythmic motion of the train allow them to

{Fig. 43} 'An inevitable part of travel by the Underground railway'

bring their filthy practice to a conclusion without even drawing the attention of the lady in question.

Female tribolagniacs are rare, and indeed poorly equipped for the full expression of this practice, but exceptions exist, and one does wonder as to the consequences of the constant and inevitable jiggling of tightly encased bosoms against male arms and torsos which is an inevitable part of travel by the Underground railway. The ladies in question have little choice in this, it is true, but experience leads me to believe that for every twenty or thirty who react with a properly modest sense of embarrassment and shame there will be one who, on returning home, uses the experience as the basis for an onanistic episode. *See fig. 43*

Trichoadoria

A unusual paraphilia in which the subject grows obsessed with hair. Two principal forms exist, much the commonest of which occurs when a gentleman of weak moral fibre allows his natural appreciation for the glories of ladies' hair to exceed boundaries of propriety and common sense. Seldom is this expressed in a vicious manner, and the typical trichophiliac is content to stroke and comb his lady's hair for many hours, a practice that meets readier acceptance and appreciation than most paraphilias.

Notably more peculiar and also more debauched is the practice of appreciation for that lower hair supplied by providence to cover a lady's modesty. A significant proportion of trichophiliacs develop this obsession, and among these the majority prefer an abundance, while the minority, more depraved still, express their penchant by cutting, shaving and dyeing. For example, the seventeenth Baron D------, whose ancestors fought at Agincourt and Crécy and whose arms display two boars, passant regardant, azure, on a field argent, employs a skilled barber so that this design may be shaved into his lady wife's lower hair, which is also dyed blue, thus simultaneously satisfying his penchant and displaying his pride in his family's ancient lineage.

Rarer still is an exclusively female form of trichophilia in which the desire is not merely for full and luxurious hair upon the head, or on the face, but everywhere. Thus we have Miss A------ T----, my only example, a lady of rare beauty but poor morals, who, when proposed to, would demand that the gentleman in question strip to the waist. Her first selection as fiancé was a notably hirsute Welshman, her second a Spaniard who was said to be able to braid the hair of his chest, and the third a minor grandee from Istanbul who, when naked, was said to resemble the chimpanzee (*Pan troglodytes*). None proved suitable for her tastes, and she at last repented of her behaviour and took up missionary work in our central African colonies.

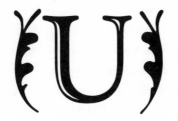

Urolagnia

A habit of such comprehensive depravity that even those who wallow unashamedly in every other form of lewd behaviour find it monstrous. Even I, who have seen things that would make many persons of lesser moral fortitude faint dead away, find it hard to approach the subject with equanimity, or even to accept it as a real practice and not some grotesque jest. Yet it is real enough, for I, with my own two eyes, have seen it done, and not by some crapulous old roué sunk beyond retrieval in the slough of degeneracy, as one might expect, nor performed upon some sorry and destitute waif brought low by hunger and the erosion of her morals through drink. No, the one time I have witnessed this abomination it occurred between Ladies S---- and A------ B-------, the daughters of the Duke of R---------- no less, and was conducted with a giggling delight I would have thought impossible in the lowest strumpet, never mind two ladies of such apparently exquisite breeding.

Reading the above, you could be forgiven for assuming that my mind has gone, and that I was hallucinating, or perhaps dreamt the entire episode, or even that I have forgotten myself so far as to tell a dreadful untruth. Pray believe me, I wish it were so, but it is not. My observations were exact, taken upon St Swithin's day of 1894, in the bathroom of Rothermere House, where I chanced to be concealed in a cupboard when the two young ladies in question entered the room. They had been drinking Champagne upon the terrace and were somewhat inebriated, while certain hints in their conversation as they began to disrobe suggested to me that they did not intend merely to take a bath. Thus I was expecting to witness a sapphic encounter of not inconsiderable depravity, but nothing could have prepared me for the sight of these two elegant young ladies, both stark naked, face to face in the bathtub, giggling lewdly as they disported themselves in this terrible manner, with not the least trace of shame.

It is my normal practice, when conducting my researches, not to reveal myself unless absolutely essential, both for practical reasons and for fear of harming the impartiality of my resulting observations. In this case, however, I was unable to hold back, and stepped forth from the cupboard, intent on remonstrating with the two young ladies for their abominable behaviour and then dishing out the soundest pair of spankings ever inflicted by male hand upon female posterior. Unfortunately I placed my foot on a bar of soap, lost my balance and fell headlong into the bath, this to the accompaniment of shrieks and expressions of alarm from its occupants. The consequences of this misfortune you may imagine, but I know my duty, and took both young ladies to task in no uncertain manner, a process that would have been concluded more effectively had not the two drunken little moppets neglected to lock the bathroom door. As it was, his Grace, the butler, M---------, and the cook, Mrs W-----, entered to find me in the process of spanking Lady A------ while Lady S---- nursed her wet and reddened bottom, so that, far from bringing home the important moral lesson I was seeking to impose, I was obliged to leave by the window.

Urtification

The use of the common stinging nettle or its relatives to provide carnal stimulation, hence the common terms 'nettling' and nettle whipping.

This is not a common practice save in rural areas, and is more often done as part of a general debauch than for its own sake, but it does have certain features of interest. It is essentially bucolic in nature, and most often indulged in by those who perhaps know no better. A typical situation, for instance, might involve a sturdy yeoman farmer using a bunch to thrash his wife's ample posteriors in order to add variety to their conjugal exchanges, or perhaps some muscular young ploughboy using a single nettle to tease his lover into surrender, a situation I observed one warm July day while taking my evening constitutional. I chanced to be in thick

{Fig. 44} I chanced to be in thick undergrowth, and was therefore able to
record my observations without risk of disturbing those involved'

undergrowth, and was therefore able to record my observations without risk of disturbing those involved.

The girl, a milkmaid to judge by her flawless white skin and voluptuous curves, lay on her front in the warm grass with her skirts turned up. She wore neither stockings nor drawers, a common situation among the rural poor, which left the full expanse of her posteriors and upper thighs on display, thus enabling her swain to apply an unusually long nettle to her skin, across and between her rear cheeks. Far from resenting this treatment, she accepted it with a giggling delight that spoke to me of an innocence almost unknown in these worldly times, as if she were no more aware of the impropriety of her situation than Eve in the Garden of Eden. Nor were his ministrations ineffective, for when he chose to produce his virile member she made no complaint, and presently welcomed him in a manner which while undoubtedly lascivious spoke more to me of Cupid and Psyche than of Satan and Beelzebub.

Less forgivable are the practices of supplying nettles in houses of ill repute and as adjuncts to the orgiastic practices of licentious societies such as the Disciples of Eros, where nettles are frequently used to excite the desires of both men and women prior to yet more flagrant debaucheries.

It should be noted that while the Common Stinging Nettle (*Urtica dioica*), especially when grown in the mild climate of our sceptred isle, produces a sharp but not unpleasant tingling sensation which one can easily appreciate might be found stimulating by those of a carnal inclination, related species, and in particular the Roman Nettle (*Urtica pilulifera*), are far more savage in their effect and should be avoided. *See fig. 44*

Vacuumism

Provides another example of the corruption of science, as it seems that no sooner had the inventions of Herr O---- v-- G-------, Mr T----- E----- and others been exhibited to an astonished and grateful world than deviants had taken them up for their own special purposes. The result is a selection of the most bizarre and improbable devices ever to outrage decency.

At their simplest, such as those provided by Messieurs F------- and C----- d- B- of Toulouse in France, these consist of a glass suction cup suited to either the male or female body, a length of hose, a valve and a bulb, these last constructed of rubber and not at all dissimilar to that system used with a photographic apparatus. Upon squeezing the bulb, air is drawn out from the suction cup, causing engorgement of the flesh, and, apparently, erotic stimulation. In the case of those gentlemen who feel that nature has been insufficiently generous in the matter of personal endowment, an increase of length and girth may also be induced, or for women a swollen state of extraordinarily lascivious appearance.

However, neither common sense nor moral propriety have been sufficient to curb the inventive zeal of those who seek such pleasures. The inventor and explorer M. E---- L--------, of Grenoble, in order that his wife might not be tempted to stray during his long absences in the tropics, constructed a remarkable device that included three distinct suction cups as well as a complex system of armatures and pistons, all of which was driven by a small steam engine. The vacuum cups, a remarkable double priapt and an arrangement of feathers would be applied to her body, with the intention of inducing erotic hysteria. Whether M. E---- L--------'s device would, or would not, have proved efficacious we do not know, owing to an attempt by their stable lad to use the device for his own private purposes, an encounter the machine failed to survive, and the lad barely so.

Vampirism

Why this creation of fantastical horror should have become a paraphilia is not immediately apparent, but it has. I myself have recorded no fewer than thirty-seven instances of carnal vampirism, but regrettably have never been able to obtain a worthwhile interview and thus reach an understanding of this curious malaise.

I may therefore offer only observation and conjecture. First, I cite the case of Mlle S----- B-----, a young Parisienne who, following an encounter with a lover of vampiric habit, claimed that she herself needed to be sustained by fresh blood and could not endure the light of day. In order to feed her habit she would wander the streets of the Latin Quarter at night, accosting passers-by and offering exotic delights at notably reduced prices. On being accepted, she would return to her room in the Rue Bièvre and, once she had tied them to the bed and straddled their helpless bodies, as promised, she would sink her teeth into their necks and begin to suck. She would then pull back briefly, inform her unfortunate mount that she would continue to drink his blood until she had reached a condition of erotic hysteria, and once more fasten herself to his neck. Personally I suspect that the young lady knew perfectly well that her vampiric habit was a luxury rather than a necessity, and sought merely to ensure that her lovers gave of their best.

Mrs D------- L----, by contrast, appears to have genuinely deluded herself that she had contracted vampirism after claiming she had been bitten by a bat during a visit to Hartlepool. Why she should have connected this particular town with vampirism is not clear, but following the incident she retired to her house and for the next twenty-six years sustained herself from the necks of a series of long-suffering maids, who were also obliged to go about their duties in an abbreviated version of a costume typical of sixteenth-century Westphalia. Each time the vampirism occurred it was as part of a long and heated sapphic encounter, so let there be no doubt

{Fig. 45} 'Mr D------ L----, incidentally, seems to have accepted his wife's eccentricity with remarkable stoicism'

whatsoever that her vampirism was erotic in nature. Mr D------- L----, incidentally, seems to have accepted his wife's eccentricity with remarkable stoicism, so much so that I suspect his own personal penchant may have been for voyeurism. *See fig. 45*

Veliophilia

The need for leather as the primary stimulant of carnal desire. This paraphilia is evenly balanced between men and women, and characterised by the exceptional sensitivity among sufferers, and I use the word sufferers advisedly.

The typical paraphiliac not only craves their penchant but seeks to indulge himself or herself in it to the fullest extent possible. Those with a lust for ladies' drawers, stockings or rubber often amass large collections or may have specialist clothing made to satisfy their desire. This is also true of at least some veliophiliacs, but a substantial proportion require no such vigorous stimulation. In illustration, let us consider three contrasting examples of the veliophiliac.

Let our first example be Sir D---- C----, of G---- M---- in Norfolk. He dresses in leather boots, leather trousers, a leather shirt, a leather coat and a leather hat, but his undergarments are of ordinary cotton and he disrobes in the conventional fashion when taking his wife to bed, bringing nothing of leather save occasionally his riding whip. I consider him a mild veliophiliac.

Mrs J----- H----, of Bedford, does not wear leather in the normal course of events, but on retiring dons a set of combinations made of the softest sheepskin but otherwise conventional, with a panel at the rear, which she will unbutton to allow her husband access to her body, something he is specifically forbidden unless she is in her leather, for without it she gains no pleasure in erotic congress. I consider her a moderate veliophiliac.

Lastly, Miss H------ T----, of Ely, wears no leather whatsoever, and shuns the substance as if it were poisonous, for while otherwise entirely virtuous, she has an addictive sensitivity that goes beyond all possibility of self-restraint. Thus, while assisting with a collection for the poor on one occasion, she had the misfortune to open a bag of leather scraps sent in by the local cobbler without realising its contents, and was immediately overcome by the leathery scent. Thrusting her head deep into the bag, she began to gasp in the odoriferous air, then fell to the floor and, with her head still deep in the sack, jerked high her skirts and petticoats, split her drawers wide and brought herself to a state of erotic hysteria, much to the surprise and alarm of the bishop and dean, their lady wives, seven other ladies of charitable disposition and the cobbler's apprentice, who had brought the offending sack. I consider her a severe veliophiliac.

Ventroadoria

An obsessive worship of the belly, this is one of the minor and less easily comprehensible body fetishes. Ventroadoria is found in both male and female, and while one might at least understand the appreciation of an elegant and gently swelling female belly, this peculiar paraphilia is almost invariably expressed as a desire for the object of worship to be as large as possible. Thus we have Mr R----- D---, of Willesden in London, who would rise each morning, spend the day at his work, then return to make a light dinner of soup and a little fish or perhaps a chop, while his wife sat down to the same soup but with copious amounts of bread and butter, followed by a rich stew or a cut of meat served with floury potatoes, buttered parsnips and probably dumplings, jam roly-poly pudding or similar, and a selection of cheeses. After a period set aside for digestion, during which he would feed her chocolates, they would then retire to bed, where Mrs R----- D--- would address herself to her husband's body, mounting up and allowing him to knead the flesh of her belly until his satisfaction was achieved.

{Fig. 46} 'Corsetiers from as far as Richmond and Greenwich vied for her patronage'

Mrs R----- D--- had, in her time, been a bouncing baby, a globular girl and a young lady of such voluptuous charms that corsetiers from as far afield as Richmond and Greenwich vied for her patronage, although in the interests of strict veracity it must be said that this story may be apocryphal. At the time I was privileged to officiate at her wedding she was certainly generously built, and I recall being suspicious of the bridegroom's motives when he presented her with a slice of wedding cake some five times the size of his own modest portion.

My suspicions were confirmed, and she continued to increase in size under her husband's ministrations, reaching a weight of thirty-seven stone and eight pounds on the day the bedroom floor finally gave way, depositing the loving couple into the drawing room of Mr and Mrs O---- H-------, who lived beneath. Mr R----- D--- did not survive this regrettable incident, but Mrs R----- D--- did, and now keeps house for a respectable family of Turkish origin. *See fig. 46*

Vorearephilia

Carnal attraction to eating or, more accurately, to devouring, for there is little of restraint and less of table manners about those who so indulge themselves. However, I have not been able to make any form of connection between this paraphilia and ventroadoria, prægravophilia or any of the other carnalities associated with large body size and great weight. To the contrary, vorearephiliacs appear to gain their pleasure specifically from the act of eating, and not its consequences.

Miss S----- J----, for instance, is a slender and elegant young lady and apparently normal in every way, save that she likes to be fed copious volumes of strawberry jam while engaged in erotic congress, and thus reaches a state of erotic hysteria she cannot otherwise achieve. Mrs E---- R----- is equally delicate of form, but her behaviour yet more deplorable, her preference being for doughnuts served spitted on the virile member of a footman while her husband attends to her more conventional needs from behind.

Vorearephilia is also regrettably common among those societies dedicated to depravity, although in such instances vorarelagnia would be the more accurate term as there is no suggestion that the members are incapable of carnal arousal without the stimulation of food. That society of wealthy but degenerate industrialists known as the Birmingham Bacchanalians provide a case in point. At their orgiastic banquets girls are frequently served nude, although not, I am pleased to say, for anthropophagous purposes, but with foodstuffs arranged on their bodies. In general, the waiters simply serve the food from the girl to the plates of the members, gradually exposing her flesh until her modesty is maintained only by a few smears of sauce, if that. On gala nights, however, the diners abandon all restraint and the food is eaten directly from the unfortunate young lady's naked skin, one of the most licentious and barbaric displays I have ever had the misfortune to witness.

As if this were not enough, the election of a new president is decided in the most outrageous manner. Girls of negotiable virtue are employed, to the same number as there are candidates for the post, and pork sausage of a style traditional to the city is served in a manner which good taste prevents me from describing in detail. Whosoever is first to finish his sausage gains the presidency of the club, resulting in a truly disgusting spectacle, following which the girls are sent under the tables with jugs of warm, thick gravy for the general satisfaction of the company.

Wackets

The mildest form of corporal punishment, whereby the extended hand is struck with a knotted handkerchief. This causes no physical discomfort to speak of but to allow it serves as a gesture of contrition, submission to the will of another, or the acceptance of chastisement. It is also occasionally used among those who wish to play cards but recognise the impropriety of gambling, with the losses paid in wackets. Herein lies the danger of the practice, for such things warm the blood and turn the mind to chastisement, so that those who are unaware of the devil who lurks within every one of us may find themselves giving in to temptation, especially if the game has been proposed by some fellow of evil intent. Thus, we have the example of a game played recently at an exclusively female house party in Staffordshire between Lady M------ B--------, a woman of extreme licentiousness, Miss W------ N----, Miss W-------- Q------ and Miss N----- K-----, all relatively innocent. Wackets gave way to smacks applied to the seat of the dress, which in turn gave way to smacks applied to the bare posteriors, which in turn gave way to strokes of the cane, with the three young ladies lined up in a row with their dresses lifted and their drawers open as Lady M------ B-------- applied the punishments with a sadistic relish. Nor was that the end of the matter, for, on winning the next hand, this wicked disgrace to the British aristocracy demanded an act of kolpolagnia from Miss W------ N----, while Miss W-------- Q------ spanked Miss N----- K----- across her knee. To my astonishment all three girls accepted this disgraceful suggestion, and matters might have gone further still had I not at that moment emitted an involuntary groan, thus revealing my hiding place and bringing matters to a premature conclusion.

Whip

A traditional implement of chastisement not uncommonly misused as an adjunct to beastliness. Whips may be divided into two principal categories, the single-tailed and the many-tailed.

As regards erotic chastisement and beastliness in general, the many-tailed whip is much the commoner of the two. While it can be an exceedingly harsh implement, as with the cat-o'-nine-tails employed for military discipline until 1881, this is by no means necessarily the case. I know of several instances of elderly military gentlemen who visit specialist houses in order to indulge their penchant either for flogging or for being flogged, both lavenderists and otherwise, but they are the exception. Commoner by far is the use of many-tailed whips of soft leather, which produce only a mild effect that is more stimulating than painful, or so it is said.

Excepting small examples such as the quirt, which is dealt with separately, even the most depraved of practitioners generally consider the single-tailed whip too severe to serve much purpose as an implement of erotic castigation or stimulation. The length of examples such as the bull whip or the Russian knout also makes them impractical for easy use within the confines of a house, again restricting their utility for erotic purposes. Lastly, great skill is required to wield a long whip effectively, but it is this last factor that maintains it as a showy curiosity within the world of erotic flagellation.

A good example of this distinctive vice is provided by Señor R------- M----- of Cadiz in southern Spain. Using a foreshortened version of a bullwhip, he claims to be able strip a woman naked as she dances without once touching her skin, and simultaneously to consume large quantities of sherry, drunk from a small, open barrel by means of a curious device of whalebone and brass that enables him to spout the wine directly into his open mouth. Unfortunately, on the single occasion

I have been able to observe this event he managed only to remove her chemise and skirt before catching her a full crack with his whip, upon which she broke the sherry barrel over his head, thus bringing the performance to a premature conclusion.

Whipping Stool

A broad term used to describe almost any device designed to facilitate the work of the flagellant, be it an actual stool, a chair or some piece of furniture specifically designed for the purpose. The term birching block is to all intents and purposes synonymous.

As is the general case with all matters associated with this form of beastliness, the whipping stool is most frequently to be encountered in houses of ill repute, and particularly in those specialising in flagellation. Mrs T------ B------ of Fitzrovia is said to have had one in every room of her establishments, including the kitchens, in case of sudden need. Some authorities go so far as to credit her with the introduction of the common form of the whipping stool, alongside the Berkley Horse. This I doubt, as the whipping stool is of a simple design wherein form follows function and no doubt is therefore as old as the carpenter's craft, a simple trestle across which whoever is to be chastised may be bent so as to raise his or her posteriors into prominence. Modern versions, designed for erotic flagellation, are invariably well padded to ensure the minimum of discomfort for the user. This may, in the circumstances, seem rather peculiar, but it is my experience that even the most urgent of masochists prefer to be beaten in comfort.

Whipping stools are easy to manufacture, and any person with even limited skill in carpentry should be able to make one in a matter of a few hours. However, for no great expense an excellent article may be purchased from Messrs J--- and G----- B---- of Ringwood. These are made of stout English oak with a high polish, padded with good-quality leather in a choice of colours and fitted in brass, including patent bars that prevent the sudden and unexpected closing of the stool's legs, which is otherwise a constant risk if the article is to be used at all vigorously. My own stool was purchased there, and has stood up to almost thirty years of use, although naturally only for purposes of legitimate domestic discipline and research.

Xanthippe's Bridle

Technically a form of combined gag and head harness, although the term has come to be used for the employment of any gag for erotic purposes. This is therefore something of a misnomer, for while history records the wife of Socrates as a notorious scold, there is, to the best of my knowledge, no evidence that he used to make her wear a gag during erotic congress.

Had he done so, he might almost be excused. While the use of a gag to enhance erotic indulgence is beyond doubt a depraved act, one appreciates that, in view of the regrettable tendency among women to talk when they would be better silent, a gentleman might be forgiven for placing such an object between his wife's jaws prior to the commencement of the act.

Alas, the debauched go far beyond such understandable uses, employing gags as an element of the elaborate and bizarre rituals of bondage and domination, flagellation and sadism so beloved of their kind. Nor are gags employed simply in order to stifle the cries of those on the receiving end of such behaviour, although this may sometimes be a factor. Rather, they are used to add an extra dimension to the travails of the masochist and submissive, and thus bring their pleasure to new heights.

Many forms of gag exist, from a simple piece of cloth placed over the open mouth and tied off behind the head to devices which hold a ball in the oral cavity, to all of which the depraved are now inclined to apply the term Xanthippe's Bridle. However, the correct nomenclature applies to a specialist device patented by Messrs J--- and G----- B---- of Ringwood, a family business long concerned with the discreet supply of unusual artefacts to those of the local gentry with less conventional tastes. This was first produced in 1861, and is modelled on the old-fashioned scold's bridle, as used in mediæval times by henpecked husbands intent on demonstrating to the world that they have conquered their wife's habit of ill-judged criticism and inconsequential chatter. Essentially, it is a cage of leather and brass designed to fit around the human head and to hold the jaw immobile. There is a hasp lock at the back of the head to prevent unauthorised removal and an adjustable mechanism at either cheek, so that the closure may be relaxed at the husband's discretion, allowing his wife to be fed, or for the insertion of whatever object he may deem appropriate into her mouth.

Xenophilia

An obsessive and irrational love of strangers or, more pertinently, foreigners. Rarely among paraphilias, this bizarre and unhealthy obsession is confined almost exclusively to the fair sex, and most frequently finds its outlet in a preference for the Mediterranean races, most notably the Italians, and the French. Why a fair rose born of England's gentle climes should find herself enamoured of some swarthy lothario by the name of Maurice or Giuseppe confounds understanding, but nevertheless it is so, and we must approach the matter in a detached and scientific manner.

Mr C------ D----- has propounded a theory whereby the travails of existence act on individuals in such a way that only those best suited survive to produce offspring. Given that what is best suited may vary from time to time and place to place, it therefore becomes logical for any animal, and man also, to show variety among individuals. Thus, while it is plain that the Englishman represents the peak of the human condition, it may be that a proportion of our women feel driven to select mates from less worthy cultures in order to sustain that variety which ensures the ultimate survival of mankind. This argument may seem weak, but no alternative explanation comes close to covering the observed facts. *See fig. 47*

{Fig. 47} 'Why a fair rose born of England's gentle climes should find herself enamoured of some swarthy Lothario by the name of Maurice or Giuseppe confounds understanding'

X-Rays

A recent discovery made primarily by the German scientist Dr W------ R-------, which I cannot claim to fully understand. Apparently it allows any person possessed of a suitable apparatus, somewhat like a camera I believe, to see through solid objects to a lesser or greater extent depending on their density. This will no doubt prove highly beneficial in a number of fields, the diagnosis of broken bones for instance, but I regret to say that it will also be used for improper purposes.

As I have already remarked, I do not claim to fully understand this phenomenon, but I will be very surprised indeed if it is long before some ingenious spectophiliac pornographer utilises this invention to make pictures that allow himself and his clients to look through women's clothes. Furthermore, we may be tolerably certain that these pictures will not only be of women of negotiable virtue who have been paid for their services, but of unsuspecting victims. The forbidden fruit is always the sweetest.

Yoke

A device designed to fit over the shoulders of a horse, oxen or other beast of burden in order to facilitate the drawing of heavy burdens – except that when utilised by the debauched the beast of burden is a human being.

The most common uses for such devices are as adjuncts to inserviophilia and to pony-play, which differ only in whether those involved are treated as human slaves or as draught horses. In both cases they might be put to use in the pulling of a cart, or perhaps to plough a field, both acts of honest labour rather than obvious carnality, but the degree of exposure involved in all recorded cases leaves no doubt whatsoever that the true aim of all involved is depravity. Indeed, in thirty-three out of thirty-seven instances from my casebooks, those in yokes, both male and female, were stark naked save for heavy work boots, which seem to be a prerequisite of this particular penchant. A typical example is that of Mr T-------- C----, who is employed as a labourer by Mrs V--- T----- of Colston Farm in Nottinghamshire. He is responsible for all the heavy work of the establishment, including carrying coal up to the house from their drift mine, which he does with the aid of a yoke. This might not seem peculiar save that he carries out his work stark naked but for his boots and accompanied by Mrs T----- herself, who urges him to greater efforts with the aid of a small and elegant quirt.

In twenty-eight of the above cases normal yokes, as designed for a plough horse or an ox, had been pressed into service, but these are not ideal, being considered both over-large and somewhat inelegant by those truly devoted to this practice. In a further four cases, all in the coal-mining districts of our northern counties, specialised yokes designed for pit-ponies were employed, but the true aficionado goes to Messrs J--- and G----- B---- of Ringwood. Their yokes are crafted in beechwood and soft yet resilient leather, with brass fittings of the finest quality, and are available to suit the male or female forms or, should one so desire, custom-made to an exact fit. *See fig. 48*

{Fig. 48} 'He is responsible for all the heavy work of the establishment'

Z

Zacchæusism

Has nothing to do with the collection of taxes, but is an overwhelming preference for consummation of carnal desire with people of exceptionally small size. Certain authorities, most notably Sir C----- V--- of St Anselm's Hospital, Greenwich, have catalogued zacchæusism alongside such blatant depravities as subligariophilia and figging, but this is clearly invalid. I do not dispute that the sight of a gentleman of three feet and six inches in height addressing himself to a lady of six feet can seem somewhat peculiar. Certainly this was the case with an encounter I once observed between H---- de T------- L------ and an exceptionally statuesque dancer, but the detached observer puts such things from his mind. At most one might argue that H---- de T------- L------ should have shown greater restraint, but he is French, and an artist to boot. *See fig. 49*

Zebra-Girls

A specific form of animal transformation fantasy which has enjoyed a recent popularity among certain depraved elements of the county set in Hertfordshire, most notably Colonel Sir F------ P------- D----.

The Colonel, a noted big-game hunter of considerable fame in both India and Africa, was obliged to retire from active life in consequence of lumbago and settled at his family estate, A-------- C----. Here, he fell in with a fast set of deplorably low moral fibre headed by his brother, Sir R------- P------- D----, who were already noted pony-girl enthusiasts and in the habit of racing sulkies and small phætons drawn by their unfortunate serving girls and occasionally young ladies who had succumbed to this peculiar corruption.

{Fig. 49} 'H---- de T------ L------'

In no time at all, it seems, the colonel had made use of his long years in far-flung posts of Empire to add his own distinct touch to these depraved festivities, first by introducing hunting, with the charioteers pursuing an unfortunate parlour maid about the grounds, and then adding to the sport by having her painted in black and white stripes in imitation of the zebra (*Equus zebra* and related species). This innovation proved popular, and before long both maids and ladies would be stripped and painted on each and every outing, although it is evidence that the Colonel and his friends are not entirely dead to the proprieties that they made a distinction between the two, with the ladies painted so as to enhance their height and elegance, but the maids painted so as to enhance the comic rotundity of their bosoms and posteriors.

As the above indicates, this painting is not a simple matter of a few black and white stripes applied in rough imitation of the beast's pattern. Ever a perfectionist, the Colonel insists on the finest quality stage paint, from C---- B--- of Drury Lane, and this is applied with great care, using fine brushes, with the stripes carefully delineated to enhance the contours of each girl's waist and belly, bosom and posteriors, according to her class, while not so much as a single square inch of her flesh is left its natural colour, be she maid or lady. As if this were not enough, he also adds striking black and white wigs, with the hair fashioned to imitate the mane of the zebra, and tails, again designed to look as natural as possible, but attached to the young lady's body in a complex manner involving the highly improper insertion of a small rubber plug, as is normal for pony-girls.

Thus bedecked, the zebra-girls are pursued through the woods and copses of A-------- C----, in all weathers save rain, which causes the pattern to spoil, on the understanding that when caught they are to be put to the spear, although it must be stressed that the weapon in question is of a virile rather than metallic nature.

Zogreophilia

The desire to be held captive for erotic purposes, a paraphilia notably more common among women than among men. For practical reasons this is a depravity seldom put into practice, but I have collected numerous fantasies, often of remarkable elaboration. A good example is that of Miss M------- M------, of Guildford in Surrey, told to me one glorious summer's afternoon when she had imbibed somewhat freely of Champagne at a country picnic. Informing me that she wished to unburden herself of a sinful secret, she made the following confession.

As an avid reader of sensational literature, and let this be a warning in itself, she had become familiar with stories in which the heroine is first captured by wicked men of one sort or another and then rescued by the hero. Like most young women, or so I would suppose, she liked to picture herself in the role of the heroine, but with the important difference that rather than being rescued and coming to marry the hero, as is the invariable ending of such novels, she wished to remain a captive so that the wicked men could enjoy her carnally.

She showed remarkably precise requirements in the details of this depraved desire. First, she would wish to be visiting the docks of one or another of our great naval towns during the later part of the eighteenth century. She would be disguised as a boy in order to conduct an improper assignation with a young officer. Thus attired, she would be accosted by a press gang, roughly handled and bundled aboard a frigate bound for a long voyage to the southern seas. Only once they were well out to sea would the truth be discovered, and the character of both officers and common tars would be such that, rather than being returned to the nearest port, she would find herself forced to spend the next two or three years serving their every whim, both menial and erotic, while she would also be subject to the lash and those personal preferences generally associated with men who spend long periods at sea.

Naturally no officer of the Royal Navy would ever have allowed such a thing, and Miss M------'s imaginings, while highly unsuitable, are essentially harmless. This was not the case with an unfortunate lavenderist, Lord S--------, whose personal predilection was also for the company of sailors, and for similar purposes, but strictly on shore. Unfortunately for him, he grew beastly drunk one night in a tavern of Hartlepool and awoke to find himself on a whaler bound for the Antarctic Ocean with no prospect of return for over five years. The experience was, so I am told, considerably more than he had bargained for, although it must be noted that this did not cure him of his lavenderism, which fact I regard as proof positive that the condition is not one of choice.

Zoomutatolagnia

Generally referred to as animal transformation fantasy, this is the generic term for the desire to take on animal characteristics for the purpose of carnal pleasure, or to have somebody else do so. This can, in theory, take as many forms as there are creatures in God's creation, or indeed possible combinations thereof. However, in the vast majority of cases adherents of this perversion become fixated on a single animal species, usually domestic. The five commonest examples, involving the horse, dog, cat, cow and pig, have been treated separately; also the zebra, which has become something of a fad among the depraved in recent years.

In addition to the above, my researches have uncovered many and diverse examples of zoomutatolagnia, the only common factor among which, other than their general beastliness, has proved to be an obsession with individual species. These have included representatives of the mammalian and avian classes, such as elephants, both Indian and African, the tapir and the aardvark, the domestic chicken in three separate cases, all British corvids with the exception of the red-billed chough (*Pyrrhocorax pyrrhocorax*), various pheasants (*Phasianidae*), the ostrich

{Fig. 50} 'What Mrs T------- thought of this procedure is not recorded'

(*Struthio camelus*), and the dodo (*Raphus cucullatus*). Nor are the lower animals exempt from the perversion of their morphology, with various species of caterpillar, slug and worm imitated at one time or another, along with spiders and numerous insects including the praying mantis and, in one instance, the sea urchin.

Two cases studies will serve to illustrate this remarkable aberration of human carnality. Firstly, Lord R------- d- V----, who had constructed a remarkable feathered suit into which he could climb in order to take on the semblance of a gigantic Lady A------'s Pheasant (*Phasianus amherstiae*). Thus attired, he would order his gamekeeper, grooms, gardeners and others to pursue him the length and breadth of his Derbyshire estate. I have been unable to ascertain the exact outcome of these excursions, but his Lordship's taste in young and personable serving men suggests a conclusion of lavenderistic nature.

Secondly, and more peculiar still, is the case of Mr A----- T-------, who was reputedly in the habit of indulging in congress with his wife while clad in a remarkable outfit designed to lend him the semblance of a lobster (*Homarus vulgaris*). What Mrs T------- thought of this procedure is not recorded.

It should be noted that there is little or no connection between this practice and the yet more debauched theriophilia. *See fig. 56*

INDEX

GENTLEMEN MAY BE INTERESTED TO CONSIDER THESE FURTHER PUBLICATIONS

∞∞∞∞∞∞∞∞∞∞∞∞∞∞∞∞∞∞∞∞∞∞∞∞∞∞∞∞∞∞∞∞∞∞∞∞

Acorns are Edible, Virtue is Vital, some remarks concerning the alleviation of poverty and suppression of vice in both metropolitan and rural Britain.
LADY PLUMPSTEAD.

Conquering Kilimanjaro, the astonishing record of the ascent of the great volcano by Colonel Lionel Trout, also of his subsequent regrettable consumption.
LIEUTENANT VICTOR L TROUT.

Corvettes and Cabin Boys, a tale of life before the mast in a man's navy.
COMMODORE SACHAVERAL SKINNER.

Curious Comestibles, a fascinating excursion along the less frequently travelled byways of dining, with extensive notes on the capture and preparation of diverse species.
BRIGADIER GENERAL SIR INKERMANN ALBERT CROOM.

Curious Comportment, the definitive guide to etiquette as it pertains to unusual and unexpected situations.
SIR ALEXANDER REDLAKESTONE CROOM, BART.

Domestic Discipline, an essential guide, which no modern household can afford to be without.
REV'D DAWES.

Ectoplasm: Form, Function and Occurrence, as illustrated by the mysterious events at Green Gables.
MISS HORTENSIA HAINAULT.

Fair Albion, a philosophical discourse on the natural advantages enjoyed by the English.
MR WALTER ST JOHN MAPLEDURHAM.

Flashing Blades, a novel of France under the Sun King.
MISS LOUISA MONKHAMPTON.

Flashing Steel, a novel of France under the Sun King.
MISS LOUISA MONKHAMPTON.

Flashing Frogs, a novel of France under the Sun King.
MISS LOUISA MONKHAMPTON.

Golgotha Beckons, advice concerning preparation for the second coming, including some important notes on dress.
REV'D BENJAMIN BLACK DD.

Heresy, Sacrilege and Blasphemy, their suppression, a long overdue study into the decay of Christian values and what must be done to reverse this trend.
REV'D NATHANIEL CROWLEY.

Introducing Cuthbert Cornelius Cook, in which we meet the Great Detective and follow him through a dozen fascinating mysteries.
SIR ALBERT BACON-FOYLE.

Mens Sana in Corpore Sano, a study of the virtues of purgatives, colonic irrigation and rhythmic exercise as pertaining to young men.
DR ARBUTHNOT ARBUTHNOT BM (BUDAPEST (FAILED)).

My Grandfather was not a Gorilla, the detailed refutation of Mr Charles Darwin and other theorists.
MR JEROBOAM DRILL.

Taxidermy for Teachers, the essential guide.
MASTER WILLIAM BELL.

The Spiritualist's Handbook, a guide to the purchase and use of such indispensible accessories as butter muslin, invisible thread and Dr Allington's Adjustable Thermometer.
DR CYPRIAN ALLINGTON.

The Casebook of Cuthbert Cornelius Cook, in which the Great Detective solves numerous mysteries and earns the thanks of a grateful sovereign.
SIR ALBERT BACON-FOYLE.

The Return of Cuthbert Cornelius Cook, in which the Great Detective solves numerous mysteries and earns the thanks of a grateful sovereign again.
SIR ALBERT BACON-FOYLE.

The Revenge of Cuthbert Cornelius Cook, in which the Great Detective solves numerous mysteries and is eaten by termites.
SIR ALBERT BACON-FOYLE.

Where Next the Empire?, a volume proposing the answers to certain significant questions as to the necessity of enlarging the British Empire.
COLONEL ANDERS BREADBATH.

Wildebeest and Wapiti, how to shoot them and numerous other species, with extensive illustrations.
MAJOR CHARLES LAMPETER.

FIELD NOTES AND OBSERVATIONS

Date   Location